MOVING FORWARD

MOVING FORWARD

Taking the Lead in Your Life

DAVE PELZER

CENTER
STREET

New York   Boston   Nashville

Center Street
Hachette Book Group
237 Park Avenue
New York, NY 10017

Visit our Web site at www.centerstreet.com.

Originally published in hardcover by Hachette Book Group.
Center Street is a division of Hachette Book Group, Inc.
The Center Street name and logo are trademarks of Hachette Book
Group, Inc.

Printed in the United States of America

First Trade Edition: June 2009
10   9   8   7   6   5   4   3   2   1

The Library of Congress has cataloged the hardcover edition as follows:
Pelzer, David J.
  Moving forward : taking the lead in your life / Dave Pelzer.— 1st ed.
    p. cm.
  ISBN: 978-1-59995-065-5
1. Change (Psychology). 2. Success—Psychological aspects. 3. Pelzer,
David J. I. Title.

BF637.C4P45 2008
158.1—dc22   2007047412

ISBN 978-1-59995-066-2 (pbk.)

To a young man who has become an inspiration to me since before he was born, my son (soon to be a college graduate, thank God), Mr. Stephen Pelzer. Live long, live strong, and always enjoy life's ride, for you are now . . . well on your way!!!!

To you, the reader. With every word of every page, I pray with all my heart for you to achieve your dreams and most of all eternal happiness. I thank you for allowing me to be a brief part of your life. For me, it's always an honor to be with you and always a privilege to serve.

ACKNOWLEDGMENTS

———⟨◇⟩———

All in all, this endeavor was beyond excruciating. Between rescue operations for Katrina, entertaining the courageous troops in the heart of darkness in the Middle East, and trying to earn a degree in criminal justice while yet still maintaining a rigorous road schedule, this tome pushed the limits. That said, had it not been for the following individuals *Moving Forward* would have never seen the light of day.

I am indebted to the following fine, dedicated folks who, without reservation, believe in the mission of helping others to help themselves:

To my longtime agent and dear friend, Laurie Liss, words alone can never express my gratitude. Thank you for being there for me, fighting on my behalf, listening to me whenever I was in a dark place, and most of all, for always protecting me.

To Kathryn Larkin-Estey, AKA Mrs. "C," the current executive director for the offices of D-Esprit, your calm presence, gentle guidance, and positive energy make every day

Acknowledgments

with you, no matter the crazies, the chaos, and at times, the life-and-death-like drama, an absolute blast. Your sense of humor makes my sides hurt! You so rock!!!

To our former executive director, the lovely Mrs. Gabrielle Norwood, for stepping up and guiding the helm during trying times and through troubled waters. You are sorely missed.

A special thank-you to Marsha of First Class Publishing Projects for her still-meticulous commitment to excellence in editing.

A heartfelt benediction to the fine folks at Center Street and Hachette Book Group USA, most especially Christina Boys, the soft-spoken editor who gave me a wide berth when needed and yet a push to better the book when needed. It was a pleasure.

CONTENTS

———◇———

PREFACE

———◇———

YOUR BELIEFS

I believe the lives we ***live*** are the lives *we* ***make***. Call it self-destiny, God's will, karma, good luck, bad luck, whatever. But when you finally sit down at the end of the day and look at yourself in the mirror—after you've scrubbed away all the grime and makeup and truly see yourself and where you're at in this stage of your life, without any pretense or the trappings of your outer façade—the reality of life hits you right between the eyes.

I believe that no matter how many mistakes we've made; how badly we've really, *really* screwed up; how old, worn out, or dejected we've become; as long as there is true, steadfast ambition, all of us have an opportunity for greatness. We all can summon the courage to deal with issues, no matter how overwhelming, painful, or degrading, that may have plagued or even paralyzed us in the past—once and for all. With determination we can stretch beyond the everyday barriers to better ourselves. Learning from our prior experiences, we can, and should, aspire to fulfill our dreams, making life better not only for ourselves but for others around us during the course of our life's journey.

Preface

I believe it isn't a requirement to have experienced a perfect childhood (if there is such a thing) to lead a satisfying and productive life. You don't have to be raised in a majestic, cherry-blossom-filled neighborhood; attend an Ivy League university and belong to Kappa-Delta-Smell-Pa sorority; obsess over having a rock-solid not-a-gram-of-fat body, thick shiny hair, surgically enhanced body parts, and blinding pearl-white teeth; or reside in a mansion behind iron gates, with a second estate on the southern coast, to obtain and preserve that certain nirvana.

(Tell me, what kind of delusional fantasy is that?)

I believe that you do not have to have a multi-gazillion-dollar starched-white-collar career, become caught up in the social lifestyles of the rich and ridiculous, or have all the fame in the world so everyone knows you *just so you can **feel** acknowledged, wanted, appreciated, and, above all, loved.*

I am of the belief that though they might be great jobs, you do not have to be a mayor of a major metropolis or CEO of a Fortune 500 company in order to take a stand for your convictions; to lead, rally, or educate others for your cause; or to maintain a vision that will pave the way for other generations to come. The *everyday* hardworking folks, God bless 'em, have always and will continue, day in and day out, truly to make an impact on their families, communities, jobs, America, and the world as a whole.

I believe with *extreme* conviction that America and other democracies like Her are places where anyone is able not only to flourish—no matter which side of the tracks we came from, our past struggles, our heritage or current social ranking—but also to rise above it all and accomplish damn near anything for ourselves and, more importantly, for our children's children. Our nation is where people of free will who find determination either through adversity or providence can move mountains and make Goliath-like barriers crumble before them. A place where fulfilling either the smallest or the grandest of aspirations is so much more than a mere fantasy, that it is a constant opportunity that becomes a way of life.

Anyway, these are just a few of **my** beliefs.

As you can probably tell, I am fairly passionate about my values, how I conduct myself, and how I treat others, but mostly about being optimistic about life in general. I hold myself to a standard. Not for pretence in any form, but for the sole purpose of knowing my capabilities. If I appear to be arrogant or all-knowing, I am neither of those things and I do **not** look kindly on those who go out of their way to behave in that manner.

I pride myself in being hardworking, caring, humble, appreciative, and helpful to others. I am, by my own estimation, the luckiest person in the world, for I know exactly where I came from. *I* have made many mistakes, screwed up really badly, and at times have made the worst of choices. I've allowed myself to be compromised, knowing full well I was stupidly, needlessly, exposing myself. I have given away my trust with the best of intentions, whether in business or in my personal life, only to have my gestures seen as absolute signs of weakness. I've chased after things hoping to prove myself to those whom I knew looked down on me and probably always would, which only intensified my futile efforts all the more.

I know how it feels when no matter what you do, no matter how much you work and sacrifice, day in and day out, you begin to believe you're never going to get ahead, that all your time and effort have been in vain. I know that at times responsibility, all that weight you balance on your shoulders, becomes too much to bear, and all you want to do is run away from the world and simply disappear.

I know how it feels to have folks view you as something you're not. I know how painful it feels not to fit in—to keep your head down, mouth shut, and eyes closed to everyday situations, *living a hollow life*, while all the time there's another person, the *real* you, deep down inside, dying to speak your piece and burst through to live life on your terms.

I know firsthand what it is like to be nothing and have nothing to the point of being nonexistent. To be teased, unwanted, and beaten down until you have no physical or spiritual strength to open your eyes just to see where the next hit will land.

I know what it's like to be used, where being degraded is a normal, everyday occurrence; to suffer from low esteem and perform tasks with a limited formal education; to live day by day with a huge feeling of overwhelming guilt from a dark past of long, long ago. I also know about being overly blessed when others around you who've experienced far worse, work harder, and sacrifice all the more are not as fortunate.

And I personally know exactly how it feels to do one's part in helping save the world, while all the time feeling disregarded and losing out on love and being loved.

Yet with all I've experienced—the bad, the ugly, and the disgusting, as well as the good, the grand adventures, and the phenomenal heights I've been fortunate enough to obtain—the single element I've taken with me and that I've drawn absolute strength from in **all** aspects of my life is in a word: resolve. To be of the belief that things will get better. That no matter how low, how tough, or how unfair life has been, all of us have the right and indisputable opportunity for greatness. The resolve that *if* we could endure the worst of times, then our mind-set *should* be that we **could** and **should** damn well accomplish anything. That no matter how wretched or hurtful an experience may be, we have to summon the strength to confront it, take charge, and let it go in order to move forward and live a full, rich life. Believe that we can not only achieve our dreams, but also muster the courage to step beyond our comfort zones on a consistent basis, to strive to better our lives and the lives of those around us. Life is more than how much you can acquire with a "look-at-me" drive to charge to the hilt with no concern or responsibility for how to pay for the flashy gotta-have-it-before-anyone-else gas-guzzling SUV, or clothes that you won't wear three months later because they're "out of style," or a closet full of designer shoes that are so outrageously expensive one pair of them could feed a family of five for a year.

On the other hand, I think it's most honorable to be content with having a few nice things that you've longed for forever—scrimped, saved, and worked so hard for—but still extend a hand to assist others who are less fortunate, an action that truly enriches our lives. We must each find the capacity and maturity truly to understand and appreciate how fortunate we are to live in a country that is literally the beacon of hope to all mankind throughout the world, while being truly respectful to those who continue to sacrifice on our behalf.

If my convictions seem a little too hard-nosed—or, on the other side, too syrupy sweet—I have sound reasons for being so adamant. Like a lot of folks, I overcame less-than-humble beginnings. As a man on the back-nine of the game called life, the more I look at my childhood for what it was, the more it terrifies me to the core. But like those who've had similar pasts, who have fought and sacrificed in wars, lived and endured through the Depression, survived a life-threatening illness, been screwed over at work, suffered through a painful divorce, lost a loved one, or any other unfortunate situation, I, like tens of million of others, quickly learned to adapt and overcome. Again, moving forward was always my key.

Now, I openly confess that for more than twenty years I've personally done my best in the arena of child-abuse awareness and prevention, as well as assisting and praising legions of others in that courageous field of saving the lives of victims of the worst atrocities. While I take tremendous pride in this work, it does not define me. Yet there are those who have typecast me as the one-dimensional "child-abuse" guy.

In my heart of hearts, nothing could be farther from the truth.

Whether it's overcoming a traumatic experience, battling tumors of the brain, or raising 1.8 kids all by yourself, it takes determination! It takes maintaining a personal conviction—holding the line for *your* values. **That** has been the banner I've been carrying for all these years.

Resolve is the message I've fought to convey in every word of every paragraph of every book I have written, books that have been read by millions upon millions of folks. Those same books have succeeded against all odds: fraud, embezzlement, and deliberate sabotage. Those books have also been fortunate enough to have broken publishing records throughout the world.

Moving forward has been the singular theme in *every* presentation I've been fortunate enough to give to thousands of organizations across the globe. In my life, I have been blessed with accolades ranging from commendations from four Presidents of the United States and being selected as the Outstanding Young Person of the World to receiving the National Jefferson Award. However, out of all the so-called accomplishments, my chief focus has always been on being a good father to my son by raising him through example (as all good parents do), while passing on these essential values that I feel are imperative.

Preface

Please understand: I mention the above only to further demonstrate my message to you. That's all. As my gracious former wife, Marsha, once stated, "Dave doesn't mind applying his fame or kudos to get his foot in the door, but only to further his mission of helping others." I don't do what I do for gold-plated toilet paper or manipulate my so-called status (which is minimal at best) to get the best seat at a high-end overpriced restaurant so I can sit next to the newest post-teen, lip-synching pop sensation of the moment. I know individuals who have those intentions, and hey, that's great for them. It's just not my style.

Another way of looking at it is that I'm not some guy who read something from somewhere and went out to become the Master Motivator of Motivation. In one word, I'm **self-made**. Like you and countless others, for good and ill, I lived it. And I'm all the better for it. Without ego, I'm proud. I've done a great deal and, God willing, I'll do a lot more. By the grace of God and a great deal of luck, I've earned my place at the table.

In the following chapters I will help you find something you once lost and/or discover a conviction you didn't realize you always had. No smoke, no mirrors, no mindless mumbo jumbo, just plain common sense real-life, apply-right-now information. Unlike my book *Help Yourself*, which went into great detail about learning how to address personal critical issues, *Moving Forward* is more of a guide in aiding you to know in your heart of hearts that no matter the obstacle, the heartache, or setback, you can overcome. That you can take the initiative, set the standard, deal with your past, and realize, that with the good, the grand, and the repugnant, for nearly everything there is a purpose. But during it all you have to take a stand. You've got to keep your chin up. Believe there are better days ahead. As my dear friend, author and Samaritan extraordinaire Richard Paul Evans (who too took a few hard knocks) once stated, "It is in the darkest skies that the brightest stars are best seen." **You** are that star. You just have to dust yourself off and have the conviction to shine and be seen!

I believe that now, more than ever, we need those who are righteous in their cause. And with your conviction, your trust, I vow to you that I will do all that I can in this cause to assist, educate, and inspire. Every word, every example in this book is for you. No matter how you think, act, or simply get by, at the end of the day when you gaze at your reflection, the reality of your life is about *moving forward*.

As I scribe these words to you, our country, our world, and our way of life has changed dramatically. I believe that now, more than ever, our families, our communities, and our nation needs, expects, and demands real folks to step up to the plate and commit to making a real difference. Whether one's best is sweeping floors for a living, getting the kids ready and off to school, or volunteering once a week at a homeless shelter, in the collective "goodwill of life" it all makes an impact. All of us can make **that** difference.

Preface

My job is to help you to help yourself, but for me to do that, right here, right now, *I need your trust*. I need you to do more than simply read this book. I need you to dig a little. To open up to yourself honestly about your life thus far. I also need you to invest some of your time. Now don't panic; it's going to be simple. More than anyone, I understand and appreciate folks who are super-duper busy. But this is important. If it wasn't, you would not be reading this book. Of course you truly desired to make a change, to make things better in order to live a happier, far more productive life.

At this point in your journey, you *so* cannot live life on the sidelines. You can't be a mere observer, hoping, praying for someone to rescue you, to tell you what to say or do or control every aspect of your life.

Appreciate this: You either live life or life lives you. *Moving Forward* will take a little—just a little—interaction on your part. At the end of every chapter I designed a series of questions to help you explore your personal perspective as it specifically relates to that particular section. I hope you become so engaged in the chapters that these questions help prod something that you can apply to improve your life. In reality this shouldn't take more than a couple of minutes, a pen or pencil, and a piece of paper to accomplish.

If you're open and honest with yourself, it will be more than worth it.

Part of the process of the Your Personal Perspective section is for you to see firsthand that when you put something down in black and white, it is much more constructive than a mere thought or two that races through your mind at the speed of light. By putting pen to paper, you are in fact stimulating your cranium as you review events of your life to put certain aspects in a better perspective. It's inescapable. Simply put, writing works.

To further help you along, at the end of each chapter, before the questions, I will reveal pivotal parts of my own life (for good or bad) and how they apply to that section.

Bottom line: As your author I am committed to help you to achieve your greatness!

So in the words of a courageous American, the late Mr. Todd Beamer, "Let's roll."

God bless.

Dave Pelzer

YOUR PERSONAL PERSPECTIVE

Your Beliefs

——◦——

- In general, do you believe that your life is guided more by chance or by the choices you've made? What impact has either one made on your life thus far?

- Even if you've made a few bad decisions, can you find the strength—muster the courage—to do what it takes to better yourself? Does your fear from your past mistakes prevent you from moving forward?

- Overall, do you like yourself, do you like the life you live?

- What do you do specifically on a daily basis that sets the example for someone else?

- As a child, as a young adult, what was your passion?

- Do you feel you have lost touch with your ambition? If so, what was the specific event that may have made you lose your enthusiasm?

- Are you now at a point in your life where you can pick up and follow your dream? If no, why not? If not now, when?

- Are you willing to take baby steps (even if it takes a few months or more) on a daily basis to move yourself toward your dream?

- What do you stand for?

- What is the singular impression you wish to be remembered for?

MOVING FORWARD

CHAPTER ONE

Learning to Let Go

Whenever I'm fortunate enough to appear for a book-signing event, I always want to give folks so much more than an autograph or a photo. I know that a fair number of them carved out time from busy schedules, and I am well aware that some drive hundreds of miles to see me for just a few minutes. So I make it a point to give more: make them feel comfortable, perform some unexpected comedic impressions, and pass along real-life heartfelt advice that's helped me through some rough patches. Sometimes my delivery is in a humorous manner, while at other times it's a bit more firm and serious. Regardless of what I do, I feel for those who may have struggled with whatever hand life has dealt them.

A couple of years ago, while at a book signing, I spoke on the importance of addressing situations. One gentleman named Joe meekly interrupted, "I know what you're saying, and I understand, but—uh, I can't—I just can't seem to do it. *I can't let **it** go!*"

As Joe stopped for a second to collect himself, he seemed

to close his eyes in shame while his face dipped toward the floor. At a quick glance I analyzed Joe's body language. By now his shoulders were completely slumped over. When I flashed a smile to cheer him up, Joe went out of his way to avoid any eye contact.

By the tone of Joe's whimpering voice, I knew he was a person who was deeply hurt, but I began to read something else. Part of me felt that ol' Joe might just be a little *too* comfortable with his sulky attitude.

We all have bad days. However, what's important to me is that we don't make every day a bad day, thus forming a negative habit.

The thing about Joe was that he gave the impression that he had no inclination to step out of his self-induced comfort zone of misery. Joe didn't want to be challenged, didn't want to deal with anything that may be threatening to him. Ol' Joe was definitely not the kind of guy who would step up to the plate and take control, in spite of the fact that *he was* in control of his actions. He chose to dwell in misery rather than letting go or giving of himself to help others when something bad went down. Bottom line: For whatever reason, justification, or excuse, to play it *safe* Joe became an island unto himself.

Yet he had seemed perfectly fine just a few minutes ago, laughing it up with the rest of the crowd when I was goofing around during my opening monologue. It wasn't until I became a bit too serious for Joe's taste that his attitude completely changed. With his declaration of despair hanging in the air, Joe exhaled deeply for all to stop, see, and take pity upon him. It was as if through the years, because he had failed to address those issues from his past, Joe had trained himself to respond automatically by retreating. He did not take action, *any* action, when it came to confronting issues, including everyday stupid episodes: a bad day, bad luck, Murphy's Law, tripped on your shoelace, lost the keys when late for work, spilled coffee on your shirt while stuck in traffic. Not even situations far more vital or devastating, such as discovering you have cancer, losing a loved one, or having a spouse deployed overseas to fight the war on terrorism, compared to the life of poor Ol' Joe.

And now, as if trying to force tears from his eyes, Joe blathered, "It's just too hard. I can't . . . I can't do it. I just can't let go of all the crap in my life. I can't do it."

*Can't or **won't*** were the words that flashed through my mind. In the next second I gave Joe a quick "once-over." I could see that he *wasn't* over the hill with just a few months left to live. He seemed in good health and was dressed nicely. In other words, Joe wasn't destitute. He wasn't on his last leg, didn't seem to miss too many meals, and didn't appear to be impoverished. It hit me that Ol' Joe was a "wallower"—someone who only feels safe, feels totally at ease with himself, while wallowing in his own self-imposed, self-absorbed misery.

If I were to help Joe, it would have to be by doing something direct and outrageous. I had to come up with something that would not only capture his attention, but would ensure that he wouldn't wiggle away from responsibility by feeding me a never-ending series of excuses, as he no doubt, in one way or another, had done for most of his life.

With Joe's last "It's too hard. I can't do it. I just can't let go of all the crap in my life" still hanging in the air, divine guidance helped me form the words. I took a deep breath, maintained my gaze, and said, "Sir, I am sorry for your pain. I truly am." Then in a more deliberate tone I went on to announce, "Knowing that you need to address your situations is one thing—and I commend you for that—*but* following through and doing something about it, once and for all, is entirely another thing.

"So, since you can't get rid of all that crap in your life, here's what I want you to do. Now stick with me. The next time you go to the bathroom, and I don't mean number one, but number two, I don't want you to go in the toilet, but, instead, I want you to go in a garbage bag. That's right. A big, thick, heavy-duty industrial strength sack, 'cause I'm sure you got a lot of doo-doo that's been backed up for a while. *Then*, since you can't let go of all your crap, well then . . . don't. Keep it. Keep it with you. You heard right. I want you to take it with you everywhere you go. Everywhere! I want you to physically take your crap with you all over—drag your bag to your bedroom when you make up your bed, to your bathroom when you shave, to the kitchen, where you can plunk it on the chair next to you when you have your cup of double espresso latte." By now the audience was getting exactly what I was implying, but I bored on further: "Then, I want you to place your bag of doo in the front passenger seat

4

when you drive to work, sit it beside you in your work space. Take it with you to the watercooler during your break, keep it with you when you go to the movies, to the gym, and on your dates, and then, late at night, when you and your bag-o'-crap are all alone, you can snuggle up next to it to keep you company."

I stopped for a second to deliver the punch line: "I betcha after two or three days of walking around with all that crap that continues to fill your bag, day after day after day, you'll *so* want to get rid of it. Won't you, Joe?" I asked, spiking the ball back into his court. After a few more lingering seconds of dead air, all Ol' Joe could do was nod his head in agreement.

I was in no way trying to disrespect or go out of my way to embarrass Joe as much as I was trying to get his absolute attention. My thought was to perk up the ears of anybody who still wallowed in the issues of his or her past—loss of a loved one, a sudden change in jobs, a heartbreaking divorce, an unfortunate childhood, whatever—before it took over and controlled him.

Now, I want you, dear reader, to stop for a moment, please, and take a deep breath, for I truly need you to take this to heart. The one thing that pains me to no end is when an element from your past, something that occurred maybe five, ten, twenty, thirty, or even forty-plus years ago (you'd be surprised), still dominates every facet of your life, causing you shame and misery as well as sucking all the esteem and ambition out of your life! I repeat, *your life.*

Now you tell me, or, more importantly, honestly ask *your-self*: Isn't that just plain stupid?

I fully understand and appreciate that dealing with and healing from situations takes time. But how much time, energy, and suffering is enough to fill the void, to move on, or, more importantly, to make things better somehow? If you're forty and still brooding over something that happened in your mid-teens, have you in fact wasted more years of your life than the event itself occupied?

Hmm?

When it comes to life in general, there is more than enough doo-doo out there as it is. Crap, crud, doo-doo, whatever you call it—it never has nor will it ever do you any good. *It is what it is!*

Do I Have Your Attention?

Now, some of you folks may be thinking: *Dave, I know what you're saying here, but giving us an example about crap—come on, now!* True, true. I freely admit it is a little "out there." But without apology my response is: Trust me. There is a method to my madness.

I could use a less visual example, but in my heart I would feel hamstrung. I wouldn't be able to make that imperative, unique, eye-opening connection that I'm determined and feel morally obligated to perform.

So that's my position and I am holding on to it firmly.

For, as you know, there will be times when you *will* be in the same position, advising or helping others in one way or another—a friend, family member, or child, perhaps. Your efforts may seem unusual and maybe not all that popular or all that cool or "nouveau," or what some folks wish to hear; however, in that role you're there to help. There's a certain quiet obligation to make an impact. That's it, plain and simple. You're not there to win a popularity contest. And when it comes to assisting others, while you can try to play it safe and not totally weigh in on the topic, or do nothing except sit quietly, stealthily, perfectly still, completely neutral on the "fence of life," hoping you don't *offend* or—Lord forbid—step on someone's toes, you know that's not going to work. It's not going to help. And it sure as heck is not going to make a breakthrough for others who may be in dire need.

As a mentor, as a leader, I say if there is something you can do, do it! If you've got something to state, state it. Think with your head. Speak from your heart. Nine times out of ten, even those who don't agree with your position, methods, actions, or words should at least respect your having the guts to try to make things better. And if they do not, well, to heck with them—it wouldn't have mattered anyway.

What does matter is applying yourself to the best of your abilities, and you can do so only by ridding yourself of stupid, worthless, esteem-sucking, needless clots of crap and stopping them from further accumulating in your life.

And *that*, my dear friend, is what true leadership is about. Doing your best while taking a chance. Taking a stand, all the while trying to avoid the cow patties of life along the way! And when you step on one of them—which in life is completely normal and absolutely unavoidable—all you can do is scrape 'em off and continue on with your life's journey without giving it another thought.

It's a Natural Process

So *now* that I have your complete attention and I hope a little bit more of your trust, let's break down my unusual example. To begin with, as you are fully aware, all of us have a certain amount of crud, slime, baggage, or whatever you label it, in our lives. All of us. Whether it's past or present situations, none of us are virginal or "spotless." Second, all of us deal with a certain amount of rubbish on a daily basis. Then add the fact that as parents, students, or everyday working folks we deal with **so** much that this "rubbish" actually becomes a normal part, a natural *process*, of our lives; from breaking an arm while playing in the front yard, to losing your homework right before the big test, to getting stuck in traffic during the most important meeting of your career, to worrying late at night about how in heaven's name you're going to make ends meet this month, it's unexpected, unnecessary stuff that accumulates every day. And you *have to* muddle through. For the most part, you dealt with it or at the very least tried to deal with it in "auto-mode," without a lot of thought or effort. It was as natural as walking.

Hmm?

Think of it this way: Dealing with mental crap from your life is kind of like your digestive system. Whatever the body does not physically absorb to keep it performing—the protein, vitamins, minerals, calcium, and, yes, carbohydrates—it gets rid of through an extensive natural process. Again, no thought or effort is involved. Your stomach doesn't think long and hard about what to do with a hamburger. It's automatic. That's what you want your mind to do with all that mental crud that piles up; your brain takes over, responding to and addressing everything *automatically*. You simply deal with it. Mentally speaking, that's how it's *supposed* to work.

But some individuals, whatever their reasons or excuses, hold on to a fair amount of that mental crud. It just keeps piling up day after day after day. It keeps amassing with no end in sight. And the more it accumulates, the harder it is to get rid of, and the more it wears us down; which, in turn, without our meaning to, programs our brains **not** to deal with situations that our minds automatically should take care of. And don't forget that all that stuff filling your head, taking up all that space, backing you up, keeping you down, is nothing more than **unnecessary crap!** Stressing over making it to the dry cleaner's in time, completing that task for your boss, getting pissed off when someone cuts you off in traffic—in a matter of hours, or days, do you even think you remember all *that* junk?

Another question (and, again, I kindly beg for your indulgence): Of all the topics all of us converse about— religion, work, the kids, the house, bills, ambitions, health, sex, politics, as well as our other wants, needs, desires—have you or anyone you know ever had a conversation about crap? Gross! Can you imagine how outrageous and completely weird that would be? "Hey, Vern, come over here to the bathroom and check out what Martha's been feeding me." Personally, I don't think that would be a pleasant experience for anyone.

And why do we not talk about that stuff? Because it is what it is! More importantly, psychologically it's not worth our time! We don't allow that stuff, that crud, to dominate our lives. It's a basic part of life, as many elements are, but nothing more. Period!

And that's what leaders, moms, dads, managers, workers, and everyday folks do. We shouldn't let crud control our lives. Every day all of us, in one way or another, have to deal with a certain amount of the stuff, and after we do, we simply move on. We cut, and we go.

Yet we allow all the psychological crud to build up and fester and take over when all we need to do is take action, by flushing it away and moving forward to proceed with our lives!

The reality is, crap is something one disregards, not gathers, collects, or needlessly clings to. Crap is the stuff you accumulate that you can and should live without! Like a smelly old shirt you haven't worn since the birth of MTV and the heydays of Duran Duran's "The Reflex." Sooner or later, all of us roll back our shirtsleeves, dig in, and do some spring cleaning. One of these days we all have to commit to emptying out that overcrowded garage where we haven't had room to park our cars since the first Bush administration (Bush Senior, that is), or that one particular closet with the buckled door that looks like it will detonate without warning every time we ever so gently, gingerly, tiptoe past that part of the house. *Our* house. *Our* world. We cringe every time we get close to "that area." We think, we pray, that by not "going there" we're safe. But that's not reality. In one way or another, all of us, whether we mean to or not, open that passageway either to retrieve something or, most likely, to throw something else in there to hide, only to slam that door shut as fast as possible, hoping it all doesn't come toppling down and bury us in the process.

And that's no way to live.

All that unnecessary *stuff* from your past you have swimming in your head that you have no control over—the guilt, the shame, the remorse, the anger, the frustration, the loss—is crap. If something negative dominates you, it's crap. If it's not working for you, it's crap. If you're unhappy, unfulfilled, and overall feel bad or dejected, it's all because of that head full of **crap**. Crap. Crap. Crap. Crap. Crap!

Think of it this way: Those folks who seem to be in good spirits and have a solid base of esteem—no matter what happens to them, or against them, they know how to deal with the crud of life.

And now that I've opened your eyes to an obvious, yet I hope sharper viewpoint, I want you to sit down, relax, pray, meditate, and open up with all your heart. I want you to really think about all that *stuff* that's been eating away at you to no end. I want you to have the courage to step up to the plate, become proactive, and flush away all that disgusting, worthless crud—once and for all!

Letting Go

As a child I endured an endless amount of constant hell and fear. As minute as it was at the time, I made a conscious decision not to follow in my abusive mother's footsteps. Yet, even as an adult, after all I've experienced, there are times and seemingly overwhelming situations that I find myself in when letting go is still a process.

Once, when I was in early elementary school, Mother had yanked me into her bedroom. As she screeched, I remember huge droplets of saliva spewing from her rancid-smelling mouth. In great detail Mother ranted nonstop not only about how horrible—just a despicable *thing*—I was, but also about how I had caused *The Family*, her family, so much embarrassment that finally Ol' Saint Nick himself had felt morally obligated to write her in explicit detail. Even as she waved the letter in my face, snapping it just inches in front of my nose, I sensed that something was wrong. The envelope had no reddened-circle postmark. The writing was in dark blue ink, the same color Mother used in her fountain pen. And the flowing, openly cursive, distinctive writing style matched Mother's to a T.

I knew.

I was young. I was limited, in so many ways. She was older, far wiser—but deep down inside, instinctively, I **knew**.

That afternoon, without hesitation, as I took my hits to the face, I cried for Mother's forgiveness, secretly craving her approval. Yet deep within my heart something began to swell. Revenge, righteousness—you name it. As a rush of warmth filled me, I pushed it down.

During the following year, Mother burned my arm over the gas stove. In her inebriated state, Mother concocted that I had committed the **crime** of running on the play-yard grass at school, thus dirtying my school clothes. She said she had been checking up on my brothers and me, driving over to watch us at recess, and she had *seen* me. It mattered not that I hadn't done it, nor that my pants were still creased just so and without one itty-bitty speck of green.

I still remember the distinctive smell of burned hairs from my arm filling the kitchen as I screamed in pain and horror.

Minutes later, so as not to expose our secret when my eldest brother, Ronald, returned home from his Boy Scout meeting, I stood in the basement garage and licked the see-through blisters on my right arm. Through a river of tears, fear, shame, and pulsating pain, I raised my right arm as perfectly erect as possible as if to place the palm of my left hand on an invisible Bible. I vowed to God Almighty never to give in, never to become consumed by hate like Mother.

As situations between Mother and me became even more bizarre, when I was mentally past the edge of bearing one more nanosecond—after I'd curse at myself, after I prayed, and after I cried deep, deep down inside, I'd picture in my camera-like eye how Mother's drinking coupled with her inner repulsion transformed her.

I knew it wasn't all me. As a shivering, animal-like child residing in the darkened basement, I fully realized I could physically do little to nothing to change my situation. But at least, at the very least, after replaying situation after situation over and over again, I came to realize that it wasn't all me. My mother was sick. The person whose eyes beamed with glee as she dreamed up new ways to torture me was not my *Mommy*. It was someone else entirely different.

Viewing the situation for exactly what it was at the time helped me. To this very day, there are still times when a wall of shame and anxiety crashes on top of me. But as with everything else, I deal with it as best as I can and it passes. Through time, a lot of work, and maturity I see my past for what it was **not**. And for what I believe it still is.

My past will always be a part of me. But it's only a

part, a very small fraction of my entire life. When I look at it that way it helps.

By letting go, I forbid my predicament to dominate me as it did my tormentor, who has since passed on. With all my heart, every day I pray that Mother can finally be at peace with her demons.

Learning to Let Go

————— ‹◦› —————

- Do you have a hard time letting go?

- If so, why do you think that is? Is it out of fear of facing the unknown? Would you rather stay in your comfortable routine, do what has become familiar to you?

- Do you find yourself blaming a current situation that makes you unhappy on unresolved issues from your past? If so, what was that event? Were you scared? Did you feel you had no sense of control over the event?

- Do you at times find yourself overreacting and striking out—physically, verbally, or emotionally—at others?

- Rather than facing issues, do you automatically shut down or deflect?

- What is your inner "safe place," and can you go there when you feel vulnerable?

- In order to live a more positive, productive life, are you wholeheartedly willing to do what it takes to replace the negative habit of not dealing with issues with the positive habit of facing situations head-on?

CHAPTER TWO

Better for You, Less to Carry

In the amazing Sergio Leone film classic *The Good, the Bad and the Ugly* starring Clint Eastwood, we find Eastwood's character in a desperate predicament. Roles have reversed for Clint, who plays Blondie, a cold-hearted opportunist. He now stands in front of a vast desert while his deviant nemesis, Tuco, relaxes on horseback. When Blondie reaches for his canteen, Tuco immediately shoots it out of Blondie's hand. With chapped lips and sunburned face, Blondie squints at his enemy, who sadistically laughs, "Hey, Blondie, better for you . . . less to carry, eh?"

Now, as unusual as this example may be, I really want you to think about those words. While I wouldn't recommend Tuco's method, his words ring true. When it comes to lugging all that crud that has built up over the years, it is in fact better for you to move on so you have less to carry.

Remember this: You will never be able to assist others— whether you're needed by your children, spouse, coworkers, friends, or parents—if you cannot manage yourself. You will never be able to challenge, inspire, or make a substantial change within yourself or those you love if you are so caught up, so overwhelmed, **and** still *dealing* with your past.

I cannot stress that enough. Okay?

So, recapping a little here, now that we've gone over how all of us can psychologically get rid of the crud in our lives, how do we come to terms with it all? First and foremost, if you have situations that **dominate** your life or hinder you from being happy or productive, for Pete's sake, seek and receive professional help! In this day and age, with all the different TV talk shows, with all the different hosts who range from the sincere to the bizarre, as well as those personalities spilling over the radio air waves, ask yourself, What topic has not been talked about, splashed all over the place, or trampled upon for all to see, hear, and gawk at? Point being: You're not the only one with issues and you're probably not the first to endure your particular situation. In fact, when it comes to counseling, there are some cities where therapy is not only accepted but considered a prestigious status symbol.

When it comes to receiving good therapy, my advice is for you to take the plunge, open up, and be honest—I mean bare-bones, psychologically naked, exposing every shred of your being. You need to get honest about your *feelings* with your therapist. It would be a complete waste of time for both parties and a major step—and I do mean a *huge* step—backwards for you if you simply glossed over events or were not as brutally truthful about crucial incidents that *still* affect you dearly.

What It Takes

Whatever you do, don't go into counseling looking for a quick fix, as if it's all gonna change instantly overnight, creating a "total new you in five super-easy sessions or less." As you are well aware (or should realize), all good things take time. If you've been conflicted for, say, twenty years, chances are it's going to take more then twenty minutes to discover the situations for what they were. You need to break down the elements involved, then rebuild with a totally different perspective, maturity, and wisdom by replacing negative, defensive, reactionary habits with positive, productive, proactive ones. Only then will you finally be able to move forward in a consistent, healthier, and progressive manner.

That's the ticket!

(All right, you can exhale now.)

But how much time does all this take? you may inquire. The answer is, I don't know. And the truth is that no one does. Not even the best of the best in the field of psychology can nail down or pinpoint that answer. Every mind reacts differently. Everyone progresses at his or her own rate. But I *can* tell you that the sooner you get to the core of your problems, the sooner you can rebuild; which in turn means the sooner you can begin to live your life according to your desires and not those past issues or individuals that seem to be holding you back or pulling you under.

Hence the mantra, The sooner the better.

You, and you alone, have to summon the ability to take a stand and commit—*truly commit*. To psychologically stand up and face those demons once and for all. That takes great courage, determination, and stamina. And doing so should make you hold your head up: At least you're trying. At least you're moving forward. And at the very least you're taking some form of action. Just keep in mind that if you have already endured those mountains of despair from your past for so long all by yourself, well then, having professional guidance can only help you. You should not only be able to get a good foothold to reach your summit, but now you can get there with considerably greater ease.

Realize that on this expedition there will be many trying legs before you reach your ultimate destination. There will probably be some sessions you will stumble out of feeling completely drained. On top of that, there may be a few visits when you leave feeling more upset, more raw, and possibly far more vulnerable than when you first came in. *Those* are good sessions. *That's* when you've opened up. That's when you've peeled back a few hidden layers. Those types of breakthroughs will eventually enable you to break the chains that have shackled you for so long!

So in the midst of all your distress, keep your cool and keep things in perspective. Hold on to the fact that *first* you have to find those destructive cells, **all** those cancerous cells, to prevent them from spreading any farther into the recesses of your soul.

(Now you can breathe a little bit more deeply.)

Not for the Rest of Your Life

A special note here: As productive as therapy can be, don't become addicted. By that I mean don't use it as a crutch. Professional therapy is there to help identify issues—real issues, past or present—for the sole purpose of aiding you in dealing with living life. A productive life. Your life. Whatever cards you were dealt, you need to adopt a "let's move it along" type of life.

Therapy is a tool, and only a tool, you apply to help you break through that psychological wall. That's it!

Therapy is **not** an instrument that one suckles off for every little "I can't tie my shoes. I fell down and scraped my knee. Ronnie's looking at me. Are we there yet? Woe is me. What am I going to do? I'm never going to get over this! How will I ever go on?" kindergarten-like episode of everyday, grown-up life.

As a mere mortal, I am of the belief that the ability to heal and move on is not a matter of a person's cranial capacity as much as it's everyday common sense. Get what you need and move forward. Press on. Considering that we are all part of the superior species, don't forget that we in fact discover, learn, and adapt mainly through our own faults and failures, as well as those stupid over-the-top fiascos. At the very least, we damn well should.

Need help? Get it. I'm all for it. But at the end of the day, the beginning of the day, and throughout the day, self-reliance is the key.

I know I sound just a *little* sarcastic and overly obvious, and to some maybe slightly uncaring. But you would be surprised what I've read, heard, and experienced firsthand. I can't make it up. It's too strange to be fiction. To be quite frank, it's sad. Or, to be perfectly blunt, it's pathetic. It's just plain pitiful how folks spend more time and energy deflecting or holding out the hope that someone, *anyone*, will save them from *themselves*.

Let me ask you this: Isn't it a little asinine that there are some who crave independence, who all the time demand respect, but can only function by becoming completely dependent on others?

Hmm?

Just be advised that it's not healthy to become addicted to therapy. That's all. The main thing I want you to avoid is being in therapy for years and years and years, rehashing the same events over and over, and still over again, with no breakthrough, with no progress, over *some "thing"* that happened years and years and years ago.

Am I making sense here?

Have you ever known or met someone who just can't seem to get over an "issue"? I certainly have. And whether they receive professional therapy or plain old logical, heartfelt advice from trusted friends, it's still not enough for some folks to make that breakthrough. Maybe those folks justify to themselves that it's safer to remain in their "cocoon." The cocoon of "Help me, Help me." The cocoon of shame, insecurity, hatred, fear, or lack of guts to summon the courage to take that plunge, that step beyond "whatever."

Some time ago, after speaking on a program about resiliency, I met the female version of Ol' Joe in the reception line: a middle-aged woman who wore the robe of dejection, unfullfillment, and "I need, I need! I want, I want!" And like Ol' Joe, "Joelene" let's say, after years of professional help, still couldn't "get over it."

In a frantic shrill she cried out, "Okay! At eight I was abused by my father, and once he smacked me on the face, and then told me I was stupid . . . I was stupid." When Joelene stopped, I thought she would continue with her onslaught. Her eyes narrowed onto mine, then, as if it were an afterthought, she exclaimed, "And . . . and I'm still being abused to this day!"

Since I was standing beside a young police officer, I quipped, "Ma'am, if you're being abused, I have someone here who will find that scumbag and introduce him to justice."

My statement was deliberate. Joelene snapped her head as if in a repetitive trance. "Arrest who? My father's been dead for over twenty years now. Why would you—how could you say . . ."

"Miss, you just stated—you just announced to the world—that you are still being abused. I never said anything about *your father* still hurting you," I countered.

"But," Joelene sprang back, "you don't understand! My father hit me, hit me right here." She pointed to her face. "I can remember as if it were yesterday. Then he said I was stupid. *Stupid, stupid, stupid.* I was abused. Abused, I tell you."

I nodded my head in agreement. There was truly no doubt in my mind that Joelene had been mistreated. At least that one time. Before she could reload with more of the same ammo, I intercepted her barrage. "Tell me," I asked in a soft voice, "how many times did this happen? How long did your mistreatment continue?"

Joelene shook her head. "No. He came home pissed off about one thing or another, I was horsing around in the house when I shouldn't have, and before I knew it my father flew off the handle. I was abused. You still don't get it—he hit me right here." She again pointed toward her chin.

Ol' Joelene just wasn't making the obvious connection that the small crowd around her by now already had. "So, you're . . . **you are** . . . in therapy . . . still in therapy," I stated in a deliberate, broken manner, "because as a kid . . . your dad flew off the handle . . . at you . . . partly . . . because you were messing around . . . as all kids do? And, again, I really need for you to answer this question: Tell me, tell the world, and for heaven's sake tell yourself—this happened how many times?"

"I already told you: once," she huffed. "Just that one time."

"So, no other hitting or punching? No neglect? He didn't touch you or do anything in an inappropriate manner?" I slowly asked.

"No. Not since that one time . . ." Her voice trailed off. "You just can't imagine the trauma. It's haunted me ever since. That's why I need, why I must have therapy. I need help. What can you tell me to make it all go away? *Help me.* Please! *Help me.*"

"The trauma or the *drama?*" I wanted to ask, but I bit my tongue. Instead of sassing off, I leaned over to hug Joelene, who by now was a little emotional. I gave her a sincere embrace and whispered in her ear eight vital words, "God bless ya, but grow the hell up."

As soon as my words spilled out, I knew Drama Queen Joelene would either slap me or erupt in a theatrical scene. To my surprise, she didn't. In fact, Joelene returned the embrace while nodding her head and replying, "I know. I know."

I then placed my hands on her shoulders and asked, "How long have you been in counseling?"

"Uh, well over thirty years."

"Thirty years?" I exclaimed. "With the same therapist?"

"No, of course not." She shrugged as she began to count with both hands. "This will be number seven . . . no . . . eight, number eight."

"And how are all those sessions working for ya?"

"Well obviously, it's not. If anything, a couple of 'em have kinda said I 'barnacle myself' to my past, that I'm self-centered and a self-saboteur. That I use my past to 'alibi' just about everything that seems to pop up or makes me feel scared. That I need to put it aside. And yes"—Joelene sighed—"one of 'em even told me to *grow up.*"

"Then do it!" I nodded back in a half-joking manner. "Really, well then . . . why don't you start taking control and become more proactive? And another thing," I quickly interjected. "If all that therapy isn't working, after all those years, then you, girlfriend—**you**—need to do something different. Quit running to therapy for every stupid little pinprick-like problem and use it only for the truly important stuff. *Then* move it along. For Pete's sake, all you basically need to do is stop constantly running to others for help. Stand on your own two feet, flush away that tiny amount of crud, and start living the rest of your life."

"Really?" Joelene asked.

And that's precisely what our friend Joelene needed to do. Admittedly, it was a plateful for the thirty-plus-year drama queen, but if she could make that initial breakthrough, it would be all downhill from there.

The *Real* Message

Now, some of you may be shaking an angry finger at me, saying, "Dave, you could have been more sympathetic to that poor, troubled, dejected shell of a lady. Shame on you!"

Puh-leez!

I don't think so. Please understand that I never advise in a manner that is deliberately rude or uncaring. Never. However, seeing exactly how Joelene carried herself, and from the tone of what she stated, and, just as important, *what* she did not say, I knew that the last thing Ol' Joelene needed—especially after thirty-plus years of therapy with no breakthrough—was another layer of "woe is me."

At the very least, in some minuscule way I addressed the situation that she kept hiding behind for all those wasted years. At least now it was out in the open. At least now, in front of a few of her friends and her own community, it was a hot potato in her lap. And, God willing, Joelene would do something about it.

Action Is No Ordinary Word

Remember, in life sometimes you only get one chance—one chance to connect, one chance to make a difference in your life and possibly in the lives of others, one chance to say what needs to be addressed or do what needs to be accomplished. One chance. That's it.

And sometimes you have to stand tall, buck up, and act upon the obvious facts of life. Whether it's for yourself or for others around you, it may not be pretty and it may sting an ego or two, but once taken to heart, once you honestly ask yourself, "Is it, was it, the right thing to do?" the answer should be crystal clear.

And isn't that a form of leadership? Leadership from within? At least **I** certainly believe it is.

Now, having an inquisitive mind, you may ask, "Um, Dave, isn't the Joelene example just a repeat of Ol' Joe?" No, quoth I (a little Shakespeare, if I may). While Joe and Joelene may appear similar, Joe's basic problem was that he didn't address his situation, and Joelene's was that she used professional therapy as a shield, as an excuse for every aspect of her life *instead* of confronting her past.

Look at it this way: Joe was sick, but would not go to the doctor. Joelene, on the other hand, ran to the doctor for every splinter, scratch, or bump and yet *still* would not take the medicine of advice that was offered!

Big difference.

Similar examples? Yes. Same pathetic, downtrodden attitude. You bet. Parallel paths, same results. So, at the very least, until *they* concede, initiate a change, and follow through, both Ol' Joe and Joelene will be lost souls. And at this stage of their lives—well, don't *you* think that's just sad?

Write this down. Stuff this in your pocket. Tattoo it on your forehead if you have to: **Don't we all live life for the simple desire to be happy?**

But the real message in all of this (and I pray that it smacked you in the face, for if it didn't, I want you to pay more attention in the future and reread the Joelene illustration once more) is in a word, **time**, all that time. Days, months, years completely wasted. All those hundreds, if not thousands, of hours of professional help down the drain. And all for **something** that in reality is so insignificant as compared to, let's say, another middle-aged person who just lost the love of his or her life, or a parent, sibling, or, God forbid, his or her own child. In Joelene's case, can she reasonably justify squandering thirty years of her life?

Think about it, and please, **you** do the math. Even with help, Ol' Joelene—who's probably forty, maybe forty-five—has thrown away more years of her life than that singular, isolated incident that, as horrible as it was, lasted ten minutes. Ten minutes of hurt, shame, fear, and anything else you pile onto the heap of despair. Call me insensitive, but with no positive results after thirty years of therapy for something that took **ten minutes** to happen, ask yourself, "Isn't that just plain stupid?"

Instead of suckling off of professionals without making a heartfelt effort to take sound advice, Joelene could have chosen to be a mentor to little girls exposed to the same situation, become a counselor or social worker, or, simply, like any mature adult, decided to flush that crud away.

Still think I'm insensitive? As an adult you try justifying all that time Joelene had, compared to a child strapped in a hospital bed fighting for her life. Or crying over Joelene's trauma compared to an average schmo who has raised a family, worked hard all his life, played by the rules, helped others in the community, and then, just days before he retires, discovers he has less than six months to live. Think of sick babies who've never had a chance to experience the pleasures or wonderment of life, or brave men and women whose lives are cut short as casualties of war. Or how about someone who passes away in an ambulance while being sped to the hospital.

Imagine what those folks could have accomplished if they'd had those thirty years.

It kind of gives the word *time* a different perspective, hmm?

Here's another line I want you to keep in your pocket when it comes to the concept of time, or what I refer to as "life management": **Get busy livin' or get busy dyin'**.

Question: Does a person truly require all that much professional help to get all this crud out of his or her system? Of course not. Historical question: With all that intense anxiety and desperation, how did people endure our country's Great Depression throughout the 1930s, only to roll out of bed one Sunday morning on that "day of infamy" in December of 1941? How did those who didn't go off to war, particularly the women, enter the workforce to build much-needed military armaments while raising the kids? How did they perform everyday tasks of everyday life *while* under strict rationing of meat, rubber, sugar, and a laundry list of other basic essentials? How in heaven's name did women, with their husbands, boyfriends, or sons fighting overseas, press on under such dire conditions? How on earth were they able to keep it together? How is it that all those folks, hundreds of thousands of them, didn't all go "postal" or crack under all that constant immense pressure?

They carried on, if you can believe it, without the aid of Ritalin, Prozac, Percodan, Valium, or any other "mood-altering," "psycho-enhancement" prescriptions. They did so without the advice or common-sense reality checks from Montel Williams, Dr. Laura, Dr. Phil, or the all-powerful, influential Ms. Winfrey, let alone without the local head doctor of small-town USA.

Not to be a smart aleck, but compared to Ol' Joelene who sought therapy for well over thirty years with still no breakthrough, how much consoling would the "Greatest Generation" require?

Can We Talk?

So how did millions of these good folks get through it all? One: They accepted their fate. They cowboyed up. As unfair, as miserable and tiring as everything was, they endured. And above all, nothing got the best of them. They pressed on. Two: To rid themselves of all that pressure, they purged. They vomited out everything. They emptied themselves. They turned on the faucet of emotions to friends, neighbors, relatives, coworkers, to those from church and other social groups. They'd meet on the porch, talk over coffee, sit out on balconies late into the evening to gab, gab, gab.

They whined, they cursed, and they cried. For some at that critical-mass moment, they'd suddenly burst out in laughter. They prayed. They revealed personal stories about how they were affected by ABC–XYZ, and, most of all, they opened up about how they **felt**. With every layer of every fiber, they exposed their true feelings.

They did so knowing full well that they could not change their past. They did so understanding that it would have little to no effect on their present situation. But at least, at the very least, they felt better. And that single straw, that one shred of *hope*, was enough to get them through. So that next day, that next event, or with that next breath they drew into their lungs, *they* could continue to fight the good fight.

They knew full well that tomorrow they'd have to get up, perform their duties, and live their lives, while all the time contemplating what challenges God may have in store for them.

Does this describe what most of America's military

dependents are going through at this very moment? Not to mention what the thousands of police officers and firefighters and their families, and others like them who selflessly serve on the behalf of others throughout our nation, subscribe to every day?

For me, *this* is the essence of life: Accepting the situation for the reality of what it truly is and accomplishing what needs to be done to advance oneself for the greater good of all, no matter the cost or sacrifice.

When it comes to those willing to take a stand, quitting on yourself, your cause, or your beliefs *is not* an option.

Time for Greatness

In part because we live in the post-9/11 era, as a society we at least "Support the Troops"—in our prayers, with yellow magnetic stickers on the back of our SUVs, or by thanking these servicemen and -women loaded down in their combat field gear while wearing sand-filled desert fatigues at airports. Whatever our politics, a burst of emotions surges through us when we are in the presence of greatness. And yet all these troops *are not* doing anything different! Not one damn thing. Same intensity, same sacrifice, same code of honor they have carried with them since the day they raised their hand in a solemn pledge "to defend this country against all enemies." Only **now**, because of devastating tragic events, the beacon of acknowledgment has shined upon them. The pendulum of praise has swung in their direction.

As hard as it is for me to state this, I must: As Americans, sometimes we are so wastefully, stupidly, and aggregately hypocritical when we judge others before looking deep into the crevices of our own faults. We see, and yet turn away from realities of life in the vain hope that "it can't happen here" or "it won't affect me." With outstretched hands we plead for others to help save us **now**, only later, with arrogance, to turn our backs on those same folks when we're safe and settled, when assistance is no longer required of them.

But with all things we can learn. Learn to do better, live better, and lead through example better. All in the name of the cause, so as not to repeat the same grim mistakes that have led to so much needless tragedy, pain, and loss.

For example, maybe partially because of how our nation mistreated our Vietnam veterans who fought so courageously in an unpopular war, we've matured, realizing and accepting how vital it is to give our respect to those who go beyond the reasonable measure. As a society, we have changed our current behavior as a result of our past mistakes, just as we need to do in our own lives as individuals.

As Edmund Burke, a political philosopher of the 1700s, once stated, "The only thing necessary for the triumph of evil is for good men to do nothing."

Am I getting through to you?

And opening up is the key. Expressing your feelings, however, to whomever—*that* will help set you free.

Can I tell you a secret? Unless some super-duper nova-like horrible tragedy happened to you, you probably wouldn't really require all that much therapy. At least not thirty years' worth.

Here's the deal: Believe it or not, I've learned that most folks punch through their holes of despair when they've opened up to those readily available to them—family, friends, neighbors, and those at work—as opposed to a professional therapist.

When you think about it, it's basic common sense. It may take an individual three, four, or even five *initial* sessions, at minimum, just to get into the routine of revealing intimate details, let alone forming a trusting bond with someone they really don't know, let alone **trust**.

Hey, if therapy works, then go for it. But those who know you best—even though at times they disagree with you and can be far more discerning about putting you in your place by being candid about some things you *so* do not want to hear—aren't they truly the ones who will set you straight, in part because of that crucial bond of trust?

Think about it.

If that doesn't work for you, here's a different avenue to being proactive by revealing issues without the requirement of professional guidance: Have you ever been at a party or an everyday ordinary event, met someone you didn't really know all that well, and for some reason just opened up? For whatever reason, you threw caution to the wind? You surprised yourself and spilled your guts thinking, *Hey, what the heck. I'm never going to see this person again.* Then in the course of taking a chance, by lowering your guard, while cutting to the chase, you found some answers to your troubles? At least maybe you'll end up with a little less weight on your shoulders.

The truth is we've all done it.

My point is: Whether it's writing that twenty-page letter you throw into the fire afterwards, yelling into the pillow at home, or just chatting with the one you love or others you know, you need to expel everything. If necessary, get professional help for serious situations *and* act upon the advice given. Either way, do something!

Take action now. No need to wait, for you've probably hesitated enough, and where has it gotten you?

If what you're doing is not working for you, well then, be adult enough to face the facts and commit to accomplishing something different.

For when you acknowledge and take action and **get all that crud out**, *that's* when change truly begins. Then, my dear friend, when you're not so caught up, so overwhelmed, **and** still *dealing* with your past, you'll be able to challenge, inspire, **and** make a substantial change within yourself and those you love. *Then* you will be ready and responsible enough to lead.

Getting Good Help

As a kid, existing as I had, everything became a *normal* way of life—get up at a set time before sunrise (without the aid of knowing what time it was), fold my army cot–bed in the darkened garage, perform chores in the garage, then more chores upstairs, run to school, scrounge food from lunch pails and garbage cans, get teased and pulverized by my peers, run back to "the home," perform more chores, wait at the bottom of the basement stairs (where I'd try to steal a nap), and then be summoned for the final household duties. Interspersed throughout the feverish pace of my day was what Mother dubbed "attention time."

My head was always in "combat mode," always thinking, always analyzing either Mother's next move or how I could scheme new ways to acquire food.

For the most part I became a cyborg—on the inside my brain raced at hypersonic speeds, while on the outside I did my best to display little to no emotion. It took years, but I eventually learned to remove myself.

I had no idea how insane my life was. By the time I was taken away at age twelve, I didn't have a clue what to do. Opening up was the last thing I gave thought to.

Within weeks of being placed at my first permanent foster home, I found myself standing alone in the middle of a darkened room. From what I was told, I was going to see someone who would make me feel better "in my head." Yet, after what seemed like an eternity, panic began to set in. Suddenly in front of me a light came on, and I almost leaped out of my skin.

"Oh, I see you are scared of the dark," the good doctor stated while scribbling notes on his pad.

So much for opening up. Later that day I held back the shame of feeling like a little fool until I burst out to my loving but overwhelmed foster mother. I had felt dirty enough about my past; now I only felt even more filthy.

It took a while, but eventually my social worker and my foster parents found a sincere, caring professional whom I could eventually open up to. Like anything, it was a process. It was all about trust. In the beginning I'd mumble a few syllables, biding my time so as not to reveal too much. I had thought I was being smart, playing coy. The Doc, as I fondly began to call him, saw through my juvenile ruse and yet was patient while still doling out pieces of advice.

During one session it happened unexpectedly. After being gently prodded, I abruptly vomited years of pent-up feelings, describing mind-numbing confusion and degrading situations. I had been so controlled, so terrified, that once, when ordered, I didn't hesitate to ingest dog defecation with worms, even though Mother couldn't see me from where she lounged on the couch in the living room. I fully knew I could have gotten away with throwing the contents down the kitchen sink directly in front of me. But after years of domination I couldn't bring myself to do it.

I opened up further during the next session, telling the Doc how anxious I felt every single time Mother would throw open the door that led to the basement where, as trained, I sat on top of my hands with my head bent backwards. "If It knows what's good for him, It better get Its ass up these stairs, now!" she'd bellow. On that particular visit, I had no idea how enraged those words made me feel. That without thinking, without meaning to, I imitated my tormentor's twisted, scowling face and nauseating voice.

With every session we dug deeper and deeper. After every session, I felt whipped. I felt exposed. I'd go home mentally exhausted.

It took a great deal of work and esteem building for me to accept the fact that I was not a *demon* child. That it wasn't all me. That my mother was wrong. That my passive father allowed events to transpire. That what had happened was wrong. That it shouldn't have ever happened.

I discovered a great deal about myself. That I was worthy. I wasn't dirty. That I was strong. That I had, in fact, endured and did the best I could under the circumstances. That my past did not necessarily have to dominate my future.

That for good or ill, I could control the outcome of every situation I faced. And the singular element that haunted me to the core was that my destiny did not have to be anything like my broken mother's.

It took a lot of effort and opening up to trust, but as I matured I saw things differently. On the outside, my esteem was lower than dirt, especially when it came to dealing with fitting in and social elements of the real world. But on the inside I continued to flourish.

I certainly wasn't out of the woods, but exposing myself while taking in the advice from counseling definitely helped me no longer to be unable to see the forest for the trees and made me feel better.

Better for You, Less to Carry

———◄◦►———

- Do you find that it's hard for you to open up and peel away all your layers? If so, why do you think that is? What are you hiding *or* what are you trying to protect?

- At times do you feel more protected, maybe even less vulnerable, if you stay in your psychological cocoon?

- Is it difficult for you to hear well-meant critiques, especially from those who know you the best? Why do you think that is? Do you automatically dismiss them as wrong? Or are you afraid they might be right, that you don't measure up because of something from your past?

- Is your life dominated by a drama that would be considered insignificant by most people?

- Rather than dealing with the trials of life, do you find yourself automatically running to others?

- What have you got to lose if you open up and let out your fears and demons once and for all?

- Is there any doubt in your mind and in your heart that you deserve to be happy?

CHAPTER THREE

You Gotta Believe

Your esteem is everything!

I know you know this. But *how* you feel about yourself literally affects every—and I do mean *every*—aspect of your life. From what you say to yourself when you first roll out of bed before you gaze into the mirror, to what you wear to work, to how you deal with the highs and lows during the course of your day, to how you act toward your peers, friends, family, and those on a more intimate level, your regard goes with you with every breath and every step you take.

Your esteem, which for some can change within a single beat of your heart, is displayed by how you carry yourself: chin held high and optimistic, smiling eyes, or avoiding any and all contact while dragging your heavy feet as if carrying the entire weight of the world on slumped, overburdened shoulders.

How you feel about yourself comes through not only with every word that leaves your mouth, but, far more vital, with your tone and inflection, no matter how seemingly small those put-downs or snide remarks may seem at the time. What you say out loud is not only heard and judged by others, but those cold, hurtful comments that swim around in that head of yours can eventually eat away at *your* heart of hearts.

Your self-regard reflects whatever prejudices you harbor against others, as well as yourself. It dictates how and why you limit yourself when it comes to trying or even dreaming of achieving what you desire—from the everyday ordinary tasks of life to accomplishing the extraordinary. Your esteem is your tool, your weapon, determining how you either confront or retreat from challenges in your life.

Think about it.

Those with little to no esteem have no passion. And those who have no passion lead empty lives. For in life, **passion is everything**.

So what's the level of your esteem? How's your passion?

If you sit down and take a deep, no-nonsense, super-serious inventory of your life, factoring in all your vital decisions coupled with your overall attitude, you'll most likely find it equates directly to—ta-da: your esteem!

Another tidbit I want you to consider: **If you do not believe in yourself, what in heaven's name do you believe in?**

Now, I fully appreciate and can take into account that life, at times, can be one continuous uphill battle, with Hurricane Katrina–like winds smacking you in the face. And it can seem that the more you soldier on, the more exhausted you become, and yet still you endure, still you plug away. You stand tall. You hold your ground. If this is you, I say God bless ya for trying. God love ya for not quitting. God adore ya for believing in your cause! For as you know, each of us, every single person on this little blue marble called Earth, at one time or another has had to summit his or her own seemingly treacherous mound of issues in order to prevail.

Now, if folks don't believe, they won't even try. If they don't try, even in the smallest of degrees, they can never draw from that well of strength deep within. So, in essence, their lives become stagnant. They grind to a halt, or, even more damaging, they lose ground. They slip. They fall. And for those who fall over and over and over again, it becomes one continuous downhill slide that lands them in the bottom of despair. For some who plunge into that hole, it gets to the point where they don't even wish to climb out.

And some, if not much, of this is due to the fact that *these folks lacked the courage to believe*! Whether in themselves or in their cause, they failed to trust.

Then there are those folks who have endured more than their fair share of troubles and sorrows. They've had to scale Mt. Everest over and over again. Those who have suffered so much it's almost unbelievable, if not downright horrifying. It's those folks, who've been screwed over so often and for so long, who have been kicked around with such intensity that they have no idea which direction they're being attacked from. And it's not fair. It's not right. It just plain sucks. But *these* folks, again, God love 'em, just keep plugging away.

Why is that?

The Big "O"

In a word: Optimism! The deepest of beliefs that things can become better. That things must and will get better. That, as individuals, we must and we will rise above it all. That no matter the pain, the humiliation, the sacrifice, or the amount of time, **we will prevail!** Whether it's standing up to racial oppression and announcing to tens of thousands of people at the National Mall in Washington, D.C., for all the world to witness, "I have a dream!" or cheesy songs that become a personal anthem to give you a boost when you're at your lowest, such as "I Will Survive," or taking an unimaginable beating like the Italian Stallion, Rocky Balboa, who with both eyes swollen shut and a face that looked like raw hamburger, knowing full well he's lost the match, still stands up to give his all for the next round. Or what about the real-life story of J. K. Rowling, the amazing author of the Harry Potter series, who at times not only slept in her car but would also nurse a single cup of coffee for hours on end while feverishly working on what some called her "off-the-wall" manuscript?

Wow! O-p-t-i-m-i-s-m! The awesome, indisputable power of accomplishment!

At any time in the course of your life, even if it was only for a fraction of a second, did the preceding examples remind you in any way of *you*? The *you* you may have lost touch with? Or the you who has carried that heavy load that life dealt, but instead of allowing it to crush you it only intensified your passions, your dreams, all the more? Is that person—was that person—*you*?

Have you noticed that those who have endured, those who have pushed the boundaries, who have held on to their core beliefs, like those mentioned above, moved on in a more productive, superior, and positive direction compared to those folks who may not have endured anything remotely extraordinary but still caved in and tossed away all hope?

And for the good folks who tried and were not able to achieve that single goal, that one golden-ring dream of dreams, they know in their heart that they gave it a shot. That they stepped outside of themselves and took that one chance. And there's immense satisfaction and honor in that.

Don't you think that, at the very least, these folks are content? That they're happy with their lives? That they're gratified with all that they've been able to achieve in their life's journey and with the path *they* have chosen?

Well, I say that a little challenge, a certain dilemma, a major obstacle or two is not such a bad thing. And dealing with struggles is certainly not the end of the world. Just as long as you have the mind-set that *you will prevail*, that, overall, you will be more than fine.

This is why there are countless doctors, both in the medical and psychological fields, who tell us that certain amounts of stress are in fact healthy. That overcoming unfortunate "events" can lead to an overall positive, healthy experience. So rather than feeling inferior, unhappy, or unfulfilled, I want you to start thinking, start building your "emotional" immune system.

Think of it in this way: *That which does not kill you can only make you stronger.*

Again, your esteem is you. It's up to you! All you need to do is believe in yourself. That's it! Just believe in the possibility of the possibility. Shape your overall thoughts, attitude, and actions as a proactive part of your everyday routine.

Enough to Get You Through

As odd as all this may sound, it's really an easily adaptable psychology. It's not brain surgery. If you're having a hard time, if you're facing a challenging situation, I want you to remember three things: 1. Don't become overwhelmed; 2. Do what you can, as much as you can; and 3. Keep your focus on the **now**.

Don't worry or stress about the next few hours. Forget about tomorrow and don't even think about the day after that, let alone the weeks to follow. Just push all that undue, unneeded stress, useless worry—all that crap—out of your head and flush it away. Find something that makes you feel safe, that protects you, and helps to pull you through. The list is limited only by the scope of your positive attitude. For me, it's that first cup of coffee in the morning, sitting outside after a long day at the office, listening to that favorite song at work, or a quick prayer that lets me vent but, more, provides me with comforting solace.

And as you're performing your comforting routine, as you're being proactive, maintain a good attitude. Keep telling yourself, "I can do this. I can get through this."

Maybe it would help if you looked at your esteem in this manner: Have you ever been involved in a car accident? Some stranger, maybe a firefighter or paramedic, rushes over and tells you, "It's okay. You're going to be fine. Everything's going to be all right." And even as your mind starts to spin out of orbit with "My Lord, my car's a wreck. How am I going to get to work, buy the groceries, who's going to pick up the kids at school?" the simple gesture of sincerity calms you down, gets you through, if only for that moment. And as the seconds tick away, as you begin to feel better, as you feel more safe, your belief strengthens. And **that**, my dear friend, is what helps pull you through.

Now I know this is going to sound a bit lame, but when you find yourself in a corner and feel the walls closing in around you and you begin to think you're not going to make it, I want you to state out loud—**not** inside your already cluttered, frantic head, but *announce to yourself*—in a convincing, no-nonsense tone, five simple words: "It's going to be okay." Spit it out. Take a deep breath, maintain your attitude, and say, "It's going to be fine. *I can do this!*"

The Base of Esteem

There are a fair number of folks—especially middle-aged folks—who, because they feel defeated by bad luck or hard times feel they have no esteem. They either believe or *force* themselves to believe through nothing more than their very own brainwashing (though they refuse to admit it) that they have no worth. In a sense, they program or contaminate their own minds, and after a length of time, just like old Joelene, it's an automatic defensive behavior. They believe that something or someone robbed them of *something*. That they are now forced to shuffle through life with the mind-set that they will never, ever be able to succeed.

Really?

Again I'm no Dr. Spock, Dr. Phil or Dr. Thrill, or Dr. Aura, but I don't totally buy into that. *How **could** or why **should*** they make the effort to get out of bed in the morning, **all by their lonesome**, *unless* they have the intention of accomplishing something? They must believe in the outcome, that they can do it, before and during the process. They believe that they are capable. They know it will take some thought, some energy, some sacrifice, and common-sense, everyday determination to achieve what they desire!

Get the picture?

Ah-ha! Got you thinking?

That's why I don't buy into the concept of a person having absolutely "no esteem." Low esteem, sure, but no esteem? I don't buy it.

And at one time or another all of us, and I mean everybody, for whatever reason or situation, has felt lower than dirt. But doesn't drawing from those real-life experiences, learning and adapting in other ways, in fact get us through whatever struggle faces us? Doesn't the experience make us a bit stronger or wiser, or, at the very least, provide us with some foundation, some form of a base to build upon?

It damn well should.

Question: As a tyke didn't you learn how to walk, feed yourself neatly without a bib, or figure out how to use the TV remote to find your favorite cartoon show? As a junior-high-school kid, did you experience angst over completing a homework assignment? Ever have to recite a poem in class? Have you ever competed or played in any games or any sports? As a young adult did you pass your driver's-license exam, or fill out an application for a job, then interview for that position? How did you do it? What made you do it? When push came to shove, what propelled you to see it all through?

Huh?

If you can perform the everyday function of walking, at anytime, to any given place, with little to no regard or mere thought for the thousands of impulses that transmit from your brain, signaling precise commands to the rest of your body to accomplish said feat—well, simply put: You, my friend, possess esteem.

Esteem is having faith that **you** trust, accept, and realize the outcome before and during the process no matter how large and insurmountable or small and seemingly insignificant a situation may be.

I don't care if your self-worth is as small as a mustard seed: as the Good Book says, you can move mountains. Look at it this way: It's something to draw from. Something to grow from. A framework to build upon.

Again, it's not brain surgery, or rocket science, but the everyday common sense of having what it takes to succeed. And here's a secret—in fact here's *the secret*: I've found that it's during those dark times, those knock-down-drag-out hard incidents, when it seems there's no way out, no light at the end of the tunnel, that one mere thought can not only take root, not only blossom, but pull you through and actually propel you to the other side.

And all you have to do is to believe.

From Your Past

Sometimes you just may have to go back and reclaim your self-worth. Maybe you have to dig deep—and I mean all-the-way-down-to-China deep—within yourself, by yourself, to retrieve what you once lost.

And if **you** have to, so what? Big deal. It's well worth it. If it worked once (especially if you acquired some of that spunk during your developmental years), or at one of the lowest, most tragic periods in your life, well then, gosh darn it, it oughta work again.

Don't ya think?

Find that well to draw from again. And again, and again, and still yet again until (as awkward as it sounds) **you** feel comfortable getting into the habit of reaching out to reclaim your potential so you can move forward.

In other words, I want you to go back and reclaim *your mojo.*

Not by Chance

As challenging as it may seem in the beginning, digging through your dirt could be the one thing that helps you climb the staircase of building your esteem, which in turn aids in achieving greatness. Your greatness. For greatness is not acquired by chance, and working for it is certainly not easy. Never has been, never will be. And within greatness there is always a cause, and effort. There is work, pain, and sacrifice. Lots. But the core of the cause, the singular element, the linchpin, is the belief in the endeavor itself. And you, my friend, are at that core.

With no belief, there is no cause. No crusade. No action. No change. There is nothing but an inert, dormant life. With belief, at least there is a conviction, a glimmer of hope, a passion. Something to strive for. Something to get up in the morning and take on the world for, to grasp and hold on to. Dynasties have been built and atrocities have crumbled on the single element of belief. Changes within a person, a society, or a democracy all began with nothing more than a bare thread of the idea of *the* possibility, a possibility.

I'm not preaching for you to go out and conquer Mt. Everest, run the Boston Marathon, or discover the cure for cancer. Heck no. But I want you to believe in yourself, in a certain cause, any cause. Just believe. To do something, anything; whether it's taking that one class at night school, putting down one soda and walking around the block once a day, or taking some loose change now and then and tossing it into that jar until it's filled and you have enough to go out and buy—you get the idea. Point being: All achievements, whether great or small, take root in the belief in the act itself.

And I know you want a better life. That you truly do believe in improving yourself. *Don't you?* Maybe you've been casual about it. Maybe you haven't challenged yourself enough. Maybe you lost your esteem. To repeat something that I want you to apply as your mantra, *If what you're doing isn't working for you, shouldn't you do something different?*

I believe you should be happy and achieve all that you desire. For God's sake, tell me, tell yourself after reading more than a few pages of this book. Don't you want to change? Don't you believe you can better yourself? *Well, don't you?*

Now, you can kid yourself. You can scan through this book and speed-read through the paragraphs. I know your time is valuable. You wouldn't get this far unless you had that spark, that true-grit belief in making things better.

Let others run around scrambling for that miracle cure-all, that newfangled, sure-fire *thing* that **empowers** them with nonstop super-duper strength so that they can go out there and do it, whatever *it* happens to be. I want you to stay grounded. Regain your vision and stay focused on the small building blocks of esteem. Think of those blocks as the stones in a pyramid, each one helping to build a foundation for the next level. Soon your esteem will become as big and as lasting as the great pyramids of Egypt, which have stood against the sands of time for thousands—yes, thousands—of years.

Think about it.

I know, it's tempting to follow the crowd. To get sucked in. To want to jump in after seeing all those late-night, inspirational, overly emotional, heartfelt testimonials, or get all googly- and wide-eyed at the latest supermarket-checkout-counter tabloid that claims this product is "new *and* improved." What exactly does that really mean? How can something be new yet already improved? Wouldn't it have had to exist before to be "improved"? Wouldn't that make it—well, not "new"? Which forces me to ponder that—gosh—maybe it's not so proven after all. At least not yet. Again, a little common sense goes a long way. Do you really think the "gorge all you want on pasta, ice cream, and chocolate syrup ten times a day **without** working out" diet is going to keep you fit and trim? Come on! And in the beginning of those programs you're thinking to yourself, *No way! That's preposterous. It's insane. It's too good to be* . . . But the more you watch, the more you read, you maybe, kind of start to think, *Hey, if these people are so happy, if they're that jazzed about it, if I can see it with my own two eyes—man, this might be it! It's gotta be the real deal. It oughta work for me!*

But the cold reality is that most of those folks on those infomercials are actors. Those photos that reveal "before and after" shots are usually altered. If this "revolutionary thing" was *such a* breakthrough, wouldn't it be the headline banner of every newspaper or the lead story on national network news? And while some—and, I repeat, *some*—of those claims may be true, the super-duper product may work for only a small number of folks who have received special *assistance*, if you know what I mean. At this stage in your life, do you feel safe throwing that much caution to the wind? Wouldn't you rather just stand up for yourself, knowing full well what you're actually capable of accomplishing?

New **and** improved—phooey!

As an adult, let go just a bit and *relearn* how to trust in yourself—bit by bit, day by day, block by building block. No hyped-up, "new and improved" bull. No airbrushed enhancement, just true life. Your life. Rely on you. Lay that road. Build that bridge over those troubled waters. Right now the best thing you can do for yourself is stick to what works for you! No matter how challenging it may be, at least it works for you. At least you have the knowledge, the trust within yourself, to choose, to live your own outcome.

And, in a word, **that's** esteem.

Perseverance

"What is your major malfunction, boy? What is it about the word *no*, the most singular word of the Queen's English, that you fail to comprehend? Does air blow through the windmills of your mind, boy?" the air force recruiter barked at me.

All I could do was shrug my shoulders while dipping my head at my soiled tennis shoes. Even though the sergeant's words seemed harsh, they had absolutely no effect on me. I knew he was overacting, that he was not upset but simply playing a role. Besides, I told myself, I had heard *so* much worse from my mother. Part of me almost cracked a smirk. "Is that **all** you got?"

"There is no way, no way on God's majestic green earth, that a stuttering, scared-of-his-own-shadow, high-school dropout foster grunt gonna serve in my United States Air Force. Ain't gonna happen. Never. Do you read me? Am I coming in five by five?"

All I could do was nod sheepishly while smiling from within.

Nearly six months later, after I had showed up rain or shine almost every day, after I'd jumped through every conceivable hoop, summiting every mountainous obstacle, the same sergeant shook my hand with genuine pride as he presented me with my final paperwork before I took my oath of enlistment.

Scared as I was, stepping out into a bold new world, deep down inside, for me there was little doubt that I would achieve my dream of living a bold new life.

It's always been that way for me. Always.

I had heard the word *no* a million-billion times. I had felt the magnitude of spiteful, hateful slams my entire life—I'm not good enough, I'll never amount to anything, I'm stupid, a loser, you name it. And I must admit there were times (many of them) when the words, the tone, the pitch of the sounds made me cringe, made me erupt in a river of tears or want to strike out in any and every direction.

Especially when it came to my social standing as a teenager. To look at me, I was below the bottom of the barrel: unkempt, matted blond hair covered my hypernervous, shifting eyes. Dozens of pimples erupted all over my oily face. Anyone could spot my haphazard, mismatched, worn-out wardrobe a mile away. And to top everything off, I could rarely hold eye contact with anyone I attempted to talk to as I stuttered like a village idiot.

Yet I had a single thing going for me: No matter how I looked or acted, or how others saw me, I believed in me. No matter what situation swirled around me, on the inside, for some reason, I just knew I was in fact good enough, that I had a good heart and, if need be, I could and would suck it up, take more hits on the chin than anyone else, and in the end **I would** prevail.

In my late teen years I knew I didn't have to apply myself as much as I did. But if it was important to me, whatever the task—scrubbing toilets, bussing tables, pronouncing the alphabet in front of the mirror in my bedroom at my foster mother's—once committed, I gave it my all. After I fell into the habit of my beliefs, for the most part, I truly didn't mind.

It took a while, but it helped when I learned psychologically to take a step back. I'd quietly observe things such as body gestures—from how one tossed one's hair, to how one walked or strutted, to how one exhaled. I searched for the true meaning of the intended motion. I read small, ever-so-slight telltale signs. I'd listen not only to what was said or how it was stated, but the passion, the raw determination, behind the expression.

I stayed in the shadows, just below the radar, but I took it all in. After a while, I could walk by someone with my head bowed in a seemingly submissive posture and I'd know, I'd feel, who had it and who didn't. Who was full of it and would cave in, and who had the guts, the true grimy grit, to give it a go and give it his or her all.

As a teenager, I was more than fully aware that on the outside I seemed like a stumbling spaz. Yet on the inside my belief made me surge with strength and worth. And ***that*** was my weapon.

It was simple. It was linear. I drew my strength from my past. In the hyper-façade, must-fit-in teen world, I'd compare every struggle I faced to that as a kid surviving in the basement. Just knowing I had gone through far worse planted a seed inside me that grew—I could get through anything.

Once I latched on to something, no matter how high the barrier, no matter how thick the wall, I'd always know I'd make it happen. I'd find a way. Whether over, under, or, if need be, by chipping away bit by bit until I'd wiggle through, I'd be relentless.

As arduous as enlisting in the air force was, it was the tip of the iceberg. I had signed up under the premise of becoming a firefighter like my father. But as Pelzer luck would have it, my paperwork became lost and I was assigned the glorious task of becoming a cook. A field cook outside the swamps of Florida's panhandle.

It took a while, but as always I sucked it up, hoping for better days. The job was as hard as it was degrading. As much as I detested everything about my task, I would still show up before anyone—at three in the morning—and stay at times until after nine that evening, only to make the one-hour-plus drive back to the barracks where my fellow, at times rowdy, airmen would keep me awake by partying until early in the morning, when I would return back to the field kitchen.

This went on for years. When I had free time, I made the most of it. At times when everyone else seemed to be in combat party mode, I'd crawl outside my barracks window and, with my feet dangling over a ledge, digest one of my various books on a particular aircraft, study college algebra, or struggle through trigonometry. My dream was not only to become an air force aircrew member, but a mid-air refueler for the top-secret SR-71 Blackbird. I had obsessed over the most radically conceived aircraft that *cruised* at speeds above Mach 3—faster than a bullet—since I was in elementary school. And now my sights were set on being a part of aeronautical history.

I knew it was way beyond a long shot. That the air force gave fewer than a few dozen slots a year for the mid-air refueling position and to be assigned to the Blackbird was a pipe dream. Still, I didn't care. In the pit of my stomach, I believed I could somehow make it happen.

As my campaign went from a private fantasy to a public endeavor, barriers seemed suddenly to spring up nonstop. From the taunting I received from those who I thought were my friends who would gleefully blather that there was no way a "field cook" would end up flying, to the constantly misplaced paperwork, it became an unyielding nightmare of perseverance. When those responsible screwed up, sending package after package after package for the umpteenth time through the daunting command approval authority for **ground** refueling, rather than **mid-air** refueling, I barely received a shrug-of-the-shoulder apology. For the most part I was lucky to receive a smirk.

"I don't rightly recall a cook that's ever applied to become a 'crew dawg,' let alone get a slot. You think after the fourth rejection in one year you'd get the message. Eh, *cooky*?" a mid-ranking sergeant once interjected before squinting at the silver badge above my left breast pocket. "Say, what's that?"

As much as I *so* wanted to tell the overweight, unmotivated, dishonorable, paper-pushing sergeant off, to tell him how it was, in fact, his staff and himself who were incompetent and the reason why I missed critical narrow windows to apply for a rare opening for an aircrew slot, I held back. The sergeant held his gaze at my silver badge before again inquiring.

I squinted my right eye ever so slightly down at the plump-faced sergeant, then in a slow, Clint Eastwood–like voice, I coldly stated, "Jump Wings."

"**You** went to airborne training? No way! You know it's against regs to wear unauthorized insignia. You could be brought up on charges. . . ." The sergeant nervously spilled while grasping for control and authority. "I assume you have verification for those wings?"

"In the package," I said curtly.

After flipping through the reams of papers, the man lowered his façade. "Well, you don't say. Army airborne training? Well, I never . . . I ain't never heard of no cook . . ." He trailed off, understanding his own message. "You know, I can't make no promises, but when I hear of a next slot that comes open, I can try to give you a call. Keep the faith, young man. Keep the faith."

"Always do, sir. Always do," I quipped back.

What the sergeant didn't know was that I was nearly kicked out of jump school. I failed nearly every segment of every exercise. I discovered I was terrified of heights, and my lack of coordination became embarrassingly evident. But I hung on. I had to repeat certain cycles, certain exercises three, four, five times more than anyone else, but I endured. Scared as I was, I kept at it. For me every obstacle simply became a building block in my determined foundation of endurance.

But no matter how much I believed, it didn't matter when it came to the cold, hard reality of time. My enlistment was nearly up. By the time my last set of ill-sent packages was kicked back, I was to begin outprocessing from the air force. My four years of commitment were nearly up. The equation was brainless: either reenlist again as a cook, or get out.

But something inside told me differently. No matter what, I just couldn't swallow defeat. One Friday evening, over a rare beer, my best friend, Roger, chimed in, "You know, it's over, Pelz. Ain't nothing more you could have done. If you had six, maybe eight months more, that would be enough to put a new package together and ship it up to Command. But you don't. So there it is. You've got to learn when to throw in the towel."

Ever since the beginning of my campaign, I would vent to Roger about every twist and turn—how unfair "the system" was, how incompetent paper pushers were, and how bad my luck was in the whole "aircrew" endeavor. Yet that night I became filled with stillness. Roger knew next to nothing about my past, nor why I was so intense. Until recently, I hadn't even known I was that fierce.

"Rog," I began, "I can't explain it. I know it's weird, but I just know, I just believe, it's going to happen. Okay, I know the rules, I know what everyone is saying, but what I feel is different. I've been through far more serious stuff. All I gotta do is find a way."

Sliding another libation my way, Roger stared through me before nodding. "I don't know what it is about you, Pelz—a lot of guys talk some serious trash and I know they're full of it. But when it comes to you it's different. With you I can feel it."

I soon came up with a quasi-plan: I would apply for a rare extension, calmly and professionally explaining my situation, how mistakes were made that were not of my doing. Then, whether I remained a cook or became an aircrew member, without hesitation, either way I would be dedicated and proud to serve.

It was an enormous gamble. But I had to try. I knew

that if I didn't I would carry the regret for the rest of my life. After all I'd gone through in my many struggles, I didn't want to have that one thought seep into the recesses of my mind echoing "What if?"

In the end it was luck, God, and something I have always dubbed "ignorant persistence." I was damn lucky not only to receive a training slot as a boom operator, but if I passed I would be stationed at the only air base that operated the SR-71 Blackbird.

Like tens of thousands before me, the first time I stepped into my flight suit I almost broke down and lost it. If anything, all the hardships, all the useless BS, somehow made the simple experience of donning the outfit more memorable.

In the nine-plus years and countless missions I've flown, some highly classified and some serious in-flight emergencies, I always knew everything would turn out fine.

The morning I deployed for Operation Desert Shield, the 1990 War in the Gulf, happened to be my son's birthday. Stephen's mother, Patsy, was more than scared. No one, not the generals nor those in the highest political positions, knew what to expect. I took care of all the things I could, from money to phone numbers to various what-if lists. Though part of me was anxious to serve and to play a small role in history with the newly uncloaked F-117 Stealth Fighter, again a calmness surrounded me.

With my little boy clinging to my leg and my arms wrapped around Patsy, I whispered, "I'll be fine. The bad guys will never shoot us down. If they do, I'll make it out before our jet explodes. I know what to do. I'll make my way to the border. I have a plan. They'll never catch me. If they do, I'll escape. If I become a prisoner, no matter what, I'll be fine. No matter what it takes, for as long as it takes, I'll come back. Please . . . don't worry. It's all going to be fine."

Patsy pressed her hand on my heart. She nodded her head in agreement before whispering, "I know it will. I can feel it."

You Gotta Believe

———— ◄○► ————

- Of all the different aspects of your life, what is the singular core belief that you best represent?

- If a situation is not going your way, will you fight for your cause? If so, how hard will you push yourself *and* what do **you** think gives you that determination?

- In the past, when an unfortunate situation occurred, can you recall that singular belief, that one mere idea, that helped pull you through? Can you recall how you felt at that time?

- When an unexpected situation occurs, do you automatically lock up, believing only the worst that *may* happen, or, after you vent and reassess the situation, do you find a way not only to move forward but totally to overcome the situation? What do you think gives you that strength?

- Regardless of the situation that you may be engaged in, can you find a calmness from within?

- At the end of the day, no matter the outcome of the situation, do you believe you gave it your best? Are you at least proud that you gave it a shot?

- Regardless of how many times you may have not achieved your objectives, do you believe in yourself?

CHAPTER FOUR

Use It or Lose It

I f you give it some serious thought—and I mean some deep, soul-searching reflection—maybe part of your challenge in believing in yourself—well, as simple as it sounds, is, maybe, just maybe, that you plain forgot how to. Don't laugh, don't shrug it off or roll your eyes in dismay. Maybe you might have lost, ever so slowly, bit by bit, over a span of time, that drive, that belief, that was once a powerful weapon in your arsenal. Maybe you, like millions upon millions of other folks, got caught up in the game of life. Maybe you divided your focus in different avenues: the kids, the housework, the bills, the car pool, the job, the gym, the diet that never ends, the significant other, the still more bills, the worry, the stress, the endless battles—everything!

Whew!

If you take a step back, sometimes life itself can be—well, bigger than life!

Now there's many a doctor in many a field, especially those in the area of psychology, who are adamant when they say *Use it or you'll lose it*, particularly for folks who may have lost their self-esteem somewhere along that bumpy road of life.

*Use **it** or lose **it***. Let's think about that. While some may blush with embarrassment like a junior-high-school student thinking it's some kind of locker-room innuendo, the motto in fact is a fairly serious one.

Example: Have you ever had a child come up to you with an everyday basic math problem and you're completely stupefied? Even though this kid in front of you is not even waist high and you have far, *far* more experience and education under your belt, for the life of you, you're completely—well, stupefied.

I have! I can remember the time when my young son, Stephen, traipsed into the room all wide-eyed, smiling ear to ear, to quiz me on a problem involving basic fractions. I became speechless. Me, a former air force aircrew member, who used math several times a day when it came to flying— weight and balance computations, fuel capacities coupled with burn rates, fuel off-load distributions, you name it, the requirements went on and on. And that was with college algebra and "trig" under my belt. At one time I was so proud I could break down binomials in my head, yet now I was at a loss to solve a petty fourth-grade homework equation, all due to the fact that I haven't used a slide rule or cracked open a math book for some time. After nine years of flying and endless scenarios, it took just a few months for me to become mathematically moronic. It's the same idea when it comes to, let's say, playing piano, sports, preparing an elaborate meal, heck, nearly anything that takes some form of thought or effort, for that matter. The less you use it, the more you lose it, thus making it all the harder to find and regain it.

Bottom line: Unless you apply yourself on a constant basis, over time things have a tendency to slip away, especially your esteem.

So what do we do to find your missing esteem? First off, relax. That helps the brain to think better, more clearly. Next, just try to recall that time in your life when maybe things weren't so good. When in fact it was a little more than tough, raw, unfair, or just plain hard. Dig deep and ask yourself, "What was the chain of thoughts that led me to believe that I might get through it all?"

Was there a situation when you were a little out of your element, when you may have felt slightly intimidated by learning a new computer program or skill, stepping out of your comfort zone to begin a new relationship, or reentering the workforce after some time? Again, it can be daunting and it may take some time. It may take some practice, but if you relax you'll rediscover that asset.

I know it sounds *so* simple, so un-sexy, so non-spell-binding, and so old school. With all I've studied, with the countless professionals I've encountered who are at the top of their field, it's the same conclusion: All of us have it. And for all of us, every single person on this planet, unless we use it, we will lose it.

And for nearly all of us, there's something from our past that we can retrieve. It's basically a matter of finding and reapplying it. Nothing more, nothing less. Again, no fancy packaging. No magic pill. No stretching your hands to the sky as you dance to the rhythm of the outgoing tide while wearing a multilayered weeks-old body wrap of seaweed. No, no, no, no! It's common sense. Tap into your past and reapply that asset.

Whom Do You Admire?

Stop reading for a moment and ask yourself, "Whom do I really admire?"

Now, ask *why* do you revere that particular person? Chances are they overcame a great deal, if not super-duper, quadruple, tremendous obstacles. They have guts. *A lot* of guts. They're not quitters. They have good ethics. They have standards. They carry themselves in a certain way. They have a certain pride—a selfless, quiet pride. They have convictions, strong ones, about who they are and what they wish to achieve. They know where they came from, the price they willingly paid while striving to do even better.

They stand tall. They stand alone. They're the Lance Armstrongs, the Oprahs, the Colin Powells, the Shania Twains. Even better and far more courageous are the everyday people: those who've battled cancer, who work dead-end jobs to fulfill a lifetime dream of putting their kids through college, who fight to protect us and save lives at home—like our police, firefighters, and EMS—and abroad when we're at war.

Obviously, one doesn't have to have a big name to

accomplish great deeds. *One must simply have a belief in one's ability to achieve.*

And for some, their test of endurance was forged through the fires of hell: Fighting off cancer, an abusive past, abandonment, loneliness—you name it. Others developed their true grit in themselves as children from challenging, if not extreme, life-threatening situations.

You're no different from anybody else. No one is better than you. No one! If you've endured something and you're still breathing, then you have what it takes to become the person you were meant to be. You just have to tap into it.

The Seed of *My* Esteem

Personally speaking, I endured some hard times, but hey, so what? Big deal. Who the heck hasn't? Again, just like you, I'm no different. And at the end of the day, who the hell really cares? My situation happened umpteen years ago. If anything, I was lucky. Darn lucky, in *so* many ways. I know that and I appreciate and respect that. This is one of the main reasons why I do what I do. I know there are those who've been through worse than I have and never seem to catch a break. Therefore, I feel that the least I could do is try to offer some form of assistance.

Because of my former situation, not a day slips by that I'm not asked **the** question, "Dave, how did you do it?" I usually just smile and kindly explain, "I don't really know how or what I did in the beginning, but all and all, I basically did what I had to do. I simply began to believe in myself."

I realize that to some folks my answer may be too simple, curt, or even borderline rude. It's not meant to be so. I also understand that my response is probably what some folks don't want to hear, hoping instead for a mystical, magical, dramatic catchphrase or spontaneous cure, but that's not the reality of "true" life. I'd rather be truthful, all too human, and humble, letting folks know that my past experience, in fact, has helped me to start thinking for myself, thus forcing me to become proactive. At the time, back then, I was simply trying to survive. Period. I didn't know it then, but now I can honestly state to you that it made me the stronger, better, more humane person that I continue to strive to be *every single day*.

Again, *that which does not kill you can only make* **you** *stronger*.

And yet there are some folks who just don't get it. **Or** maybe there are some individuals who don't *wish* to get it.

Over the last fifteen-plus years, I've been fortunate to be interviewed by just about everyone in the business, and I do mean everyone. From Oprah, to Larry King, to half a dozen appearances with Montel Williams, to hundreds upon hundreds of radios shows and magazines and papers from coast to coast, as well as around the globe. And while most of these seasoned professionals seem to understand my plight at the time, some, despite their vast experience and position, cannot seem to grasp the simple answer to their question. More than once I have had an ultra-A-list celebrity television host excitedly inquire with wide eyes (you're not going to believe this), "David Pelzer, wow! What an amazing story! So, as a tiny, helpless, frightened child when you were going through all that horrible, disgusting, gut-wrenching abuse, what was it exactly that you read that helped you?" Or, "Did you attend a motivational retreat? Did you have a life coach? Tell me, tell the audience, was there an episode from *my* show that did it for you?"

(Oh ma Gawd!)

I know I'm flogging a dead horse here, but as they say, the floggings will continue until morale improves. For there are indeed some people, from all walks of life, who, no matter what you say, what you do, or how you live your life, cannot grasp a common, rather simple, non-cosmic solution to an uncommon situation. Many of those who have realized great accomplishments and awe-inspiring achievements **began** with the bare, hair-thin-thread belief that maybe, just maybe, things might get better. Maybe things might work out, but regardless of the results, the true belief in the cause itself was well worth the effort.

With every interview and audience I've been fortunate enough to address—whether major corporations, school assemblies, universities, specialized in-service training, or appearances at countless book signings—I do my best to ensure that folks *get* "the message." The message of resilience. The message of not only overcoming problems and achieving a certain stature, but also the desire still to step beyond and try, at the very least, to attain a certain greatness. And if there are any doubts within you, I pray that, after reading a few of the following examples, you will "get it" as well.

There are prominent, important turning points in all of our lives. Mine, for good or ill, just like millions of folks before me, transpired through devastating circumstances. I was fortunate to be able to recognize, harness, and then apply my foundation of esteem to build upon throughout my life. And you, God love ya, are no different.

By the time I was eight years old I had become conditioned. I knew my place within the food chain of life. By then, Mother was in the full swing of her own misery: the nonstop drinking, the crumbling façade of the Brady Bunch–type marriage, and whatever demons buried from her past that seemed to surface from the depths of her troubled soul and ignite.

As I talked about earlier in the personal perspectives, as a child I knew the special rules that applied only to me. I was The Boy. I was not a member of The Family. I was not to be addressed, looked upon, or even acknowledged. I was, for all intents and purposes, invisible. God help my brothers, Ron and Stan, if they even whispered hello or tried to sneak me a piece of bread.

I was a troll-like slave who lived in the basement, at night sleeping on a worn canvas army cot, and during the day trembling at the bottom of the stairs with fear while awaiting Mother's next summons.

In my concrete, black-and-white mind, I fought with myself to understand the "why?" The "what?" The one horrible, hideous thing I had done wrong. I had spent endless hours contemplating "what" I could do or undo to make Mother happy, to redeem myself somehow in the hopes that it would allow me to return as a member of The Family. *Her family.*

After I turned seven, things began happening too fast. Events were spinning out of control. The once-in-a-while "treatment" became an everyday occurrence, then began happening several times a day. I had fantasized that my beautiful, Snow White–like mother would one day wake up from her drunken, angered slumber. But eventually I had to accept the cold, hard fact that things would not get any better for me. Overall, I was alone with myself.

One afternoon, I must have either disobeyed a command—looked up into Mother's eyes without permission, not met a time limit for one of my chores, or the worst crime: gotten caught stealing food from the kitchen garbage can. Whatever the offense, a thrashing followed and I ended up at the bottom of the dark stairs as silver spots floated in front of my eyes. I do remember that the pain was unbearable. I was scared. I was tired. And I was just plain worn out from the non-stop degenerating way of existence. So, as The Family happily ate (as Mother was truly the best cook) upstairs, I whimpered to myself until my tears ran dry. The pain came in throbbing waves, from my toes to my nose. I couldn't shake it.

Without really thinking, I fought to control my heaving chest after crying. So I counted to myself. I slowly counted backwards from sixty. I calmly visualized the bold white numbers that I played inside my head. When I reached the number one, I took in another deep breath and started again. Then again, and again, and yet again. I can truthfully state that with every passing minute, while the pain still seared throughout my body, somehow it just wasn't as bad as it had been a mere sixty seconds ago.

It was then that it hit me. "Hey," I told myself, "if I can survive the pain from a few minutes ago, then I know I can get through the next few minutes . . . that won't be quite so bad." In other words, I announced to myself, "I can do this! I can get through *this*. I'm gonna be okay."

Here's a truth about life: None of us know what tomorrow holds. Neither can we begin to contemplate what God has in store for us. But with every day and every situation, at the very least we have to have the faith that we can make it through, that we're going to be okay. Tragedies strike and bad situations spring up from nowhere. When they do, we have to reclaim what may be lost: the indisputable belief in ourselves. That we're gonna be okay.

And while some may shake their head in disbelief at my simple solution to my former situation in the basement, I pose a few questions: *Where's your thread of belief? Do you confront your challenges? Do you have what it takes to see things through?* After all the chest beating and tough talk in front of others to make yourself look or feel superior, when you're all alone, do you still think you can pull it off? Or will you silently retreat within yourself, make yet another excuse while hoping those who know you will forget your latest escape from facing your reality?

Well?

I don't care who you are or who you're not. How much money you have or don't have. I don't give a darn if you're overly glamorous or plain Jane, whether you have raw skin or a perfect complexion, if you're overweight, underweight, have it all, or have nothing. Whether you've made a few mistakes (who the heck hasn't?) or really, *really* screwed up. If you have the guts to stand up for yourself, fight the good fight, and have a true commitment to your cause, you've sure as hell got my vote.

If you've lost your thread of esteem, stand up for yourself. Quit quitting on you. Grow up, cowboy up, find it, nurture it, and put it to the test. Make it take root and watch it grow, grow, grow.

I admit that counting backwards to help me take my mind off the searing pain and never-ending degradation was certainly not the cure. But that one component provided me with an opportunity to believe in myself. Again, no mind-numbing answer to the cosmos, but for me it was that fleeting white star that I could harness from the vast emptiness of my dark world.

Capturing *and* nurturing that single element gave me a needed boost to my morale. As insignificant as it was, it was more, so much more, than I had before. It gave me something to draw from for the next time and the next *and* the next.

I'm sure that I sound foolish to some folks. But at least during that dark time in my life, alone, as a terrified, shivering child in the darkness, that one element blossomed into a belief in the possibility of surviving.

That one speck of esteem helped immensely when Mother would fill up a bathtub with cold water and humiliate me by having me lie with my nose barely above the cold water for all to see and gawk at. Later, as the water slowly seeped down the drain, I'd begin to shiver uncontrollably. Terrified of being caught moving my hands under my legs or into the pits of my arms to warm myself, I lay perfectly still. I didn't dare to think of springing out of the tub and grabbing a towel. I never even thought of disobeying Mother's instructions. I wanted to disappear. I so wanted to scream, to cry away the cold, to disassociate myself from yet another humiliation.

But then I calmed myself. Automatically I'd tell myself, *I can get through this*. With my eyes locked on the bathroom ceiling, I began to replay the numbers in my head. I made sure to focus on every clear-cut number that flashed through my mind. Then, ever so slowly, I paid careful attention to my pacing. I maintained a certain rhythm, not counting too fast or too slow. As my body shivered and my teeth chattered during the first minute, the next was not as severe. As the minutes slid by, I didn't exactly feel warmer, but I knew I would get through the worst of it.

Now, many folks might cry out, "That's a pretty weird way of building one's esteem." And my instant reply is yes it is, but all in all, some things are discovered in the most unusual places and most horrid of circumstances. As long as you discover the root of your self-esteem and cultivate it, that's all I'm concerned about.

What does counting have to do with one's self-esteem? For me counting was a mechanism, a bridge, that led me to believe I could survive. If I could do that, *I believed I could accomplish anything.*

We all know that in Normalville, USA, one's esteem is developed by one's family values, in elementary sports, or menial challenges. But as you know, life is not always Normalville, USA. Life can be drastic. Life can be extreme. So you use what you can, when you can, as you can. You make the best of things. And no matter what, you keep the faith within yourself.

Keeping the Faith

I don't care how long ago or insignificant events in your life may seem to you, it was that first step of blind, raw faith that became the one thing that guided you through the dark portal. With every day and with every step, your faith is the foundation of your life's journey.

To restate for the umpteenth time, I am in no way trying to proclaim that you must have endured some appalling episode, nor am I saying that you have to become Super Person, flying through the air with a flashy, fluttering, bright red, bullet-proof cape. I only wish for you to come to the realization that at the very least, your belief is an enormous asset in your arsenal of dealing with life. Your esteem silently waits for you to don it whenever needed.

I am no different from anyone else; I lose it from time to time. To this very day, whenever I face a serious issue, whenever I become scared or feel I just cannot make it, when I feel I don't have the strength or the time it takes to dedicate to a certain cause, I have the quiet faith that originated from far more grave situations. And it's that belief that pulls me through.

At the end of the day, I pray, I recalculate, I evaluate, and I try yet again. I maintain a quiet faith in better days ahead.

And now it's your time. Your time to stand up and shine, to seek out bigger horizons, to take charge and take hold. At the very least, you have to have the belief—the true belief—in yourself. Events will swirl around you and *seem* out of control, but with your unshakable faith, you, my friend, will be able to weather the storm. Any storm!

Try this: From this moment on, I want you to be conscious of your walk, your body language, the tone of your voice, what you say for the world to hear, and, most importantly, what you say that only you and God know. Be self-aware, and while doing so keep with you an ounce of faith. Be consistent and give it a little time, and then watch your world unfold.

Never forget, your esteem is what makes you who you are. For you have been and always will be the total sum of the faith that you carry deep within!

Just a Thread

"Hey, didn't you *use* to be Dave Pelzer?"

Upon hearing the words, all I could do was retreat farther into my fragile shell. Part of me wanted to scream, "Bug off!" but since moving to the Palm Springs area over four years earlier, George, a fellow cigar aficionado, and I had become close friends.

Sitting down beside me, he shook his head. "You're going to be fine. You're going to get through this."

"Yeah," I wanted to sneer, "what the hell do you know?" I could feel the combination of intense anger and anguish surge through my body. I wanted to find a place to throw up, something to hit, and a place to lie down, all at once.

"If anybody can get through this, it's you, my friend," George confided. Then, before leaving me be, he added, "I'm not trying to sound cruel, and I don't wish to seem callous, but keep in mind—it's only a divorce."

It had been months since Marsha, my second wife, and I had filed for divorce. Since that day everything about my life had come crashing down. We had known each other for nine years and were married for over five. We were a team. The team. Mar was director for the entire business, while I wrote the books and traveled abroad. But in the end, it all became more than we could both bear: Marsha longing to live near her ailing parents in Georgia while I wanted to stay in California to be near my son; working side by side in the high-speed, never-yielding, intense, save-the-world environment; me being on the road putting in sixteen-plus-hour workdays over 200 days out of the year.

We tried. Marsha more than I. But we had passed a point of no return. As much as we once loved *and* still loved each other, sadly, we were not the same couple we once had been.

When I lost Marsha, I lost my world. I lost my faith. I so prided myself on doing my best, giving my all to others, sometimes under the most horrific, unmentionable, disgusting circumstances, yet without meaning to I'd return home at times with little left to devote to my wife.

As I sat on the bench in the cigar shop, all I could do was cup my trembling hands. My mind, my body, and my spirit were beyond the edge of a total collapse. On average, I was lucky to sleep ninety minutes a day. I could barely keep any food down and if I did, I was on the toilet in a matter of minutes. My weight, once steady at 180-plus, now hovered just above 160 pounds. At times I'd forget to shave, and my eyes became sunken and vacant. When I walked, my shoulders slumped forward, keeping my head bent down.

For a person who kept emotions shut down and buried deep for so many years, I was now experiencing a nonstop range of feelings like never before: longing, betrayal, anger, abandonment, and complete sorrow. When I married Marsha, I had married her for life.

Whatever mistakes or downright screwups I had made with Stephen's mother, I had been determined not to repeat with Marsha. With Mar I truly gave it my all. She was more than my wife; Marsha was my world, she was my everything. And I planned all that I could around my wife, from exotic vacations that were blueprinted a full year in advance, to arranging the entire house with her favorite flowers, to driving her six hours nonstop in the middle of the night to beautiful Carmel while she slept (even though I myself had been up for days and had just returned from being on the road), to cooking a romantic dinner—I loved doing things for Marsha.

While my business life was structured with several events every day to the most minute minute, which at times drove me completely crazy, with Mar I loved nothing more than being at home with her. I'd get up early, take care of the doggies, work out at the gym, then put in a furious day at work, all the while watching the clock, counting down the time when I could make Marsha her special martini and the two of us could just be together.

We gabbed. We fantasized. We planned. From how long Mar wished to stay when we visited France (her childhood dream), to how much longer my body could physically endure all the traveling. When Marsha first uttered the "R" word—Retire—I froze. I had never given it a single thought, but the more we explored slowing down and all that we could do as a couple, the more secure I began to feel about my future.

And now, through a life-altering chain of events, I had absolutely no idea what or if I would even eat for my next meal, let alone projecting anything significant involving how I would live the rest of my life. At times I actually fantasized about finding a cliff to roar off of, and I might have if it hadn't been for my still-structured work schedule.

Even months after the separation, I felt like my soul was empty to the core. I slowly became convinced that I couldn't get through it. That I would forever be sickly and unwanted, and end up old and alone.

As much as I prayed, cried, and yelled, the intense pain and shame still wouldn't subside. At times, late into the night, I'd wander around the empty house, clutching photos of Marsha and me together. In the beginning the sensation was ever so slight, but I'd slowly feel a crushing band squeeze my chest. I'd end up either falling to my knees or trying to find a chair to collapse in, fighting to draw in some oxygen.

One night, after experiencing the built-up pressure, before my frantic, exhausted mind spun out of control, I leaned my head back and closed my eyes. With the tension increasing ever so slightly around my torso, instead of panicking I found a rhythm. I counted to myself. With my eyes clamped shut, I visualized bold white numbers clicking backwards from 10 to 1. Then, like I had before when I was degraded as a child and forced to lie in the cold-water-filled bathtub shaking like a leaf, I repeated the cycle. In a moment of clarity, I rediscovered the same simple thread I had applied when my life *was* at extreme risk, back then I *was* completely alone.

That night I sat on the living room floor for more than an hour just counting backwards. I slowed down. I regained a sense of control. I convinced myself that if I could get through the next ten seconds, it would be more than before. That I'd be fine. When that didn't seem so bad, I'd tell myself, "Come on—a minute, just get through the next minute. Do it. Come on—you'll be fine!"

Reapplying that element from my past helped me immensely. Something from over thirty years ago that I had completely forgotten about helped me turn the corner. It certainly wasn't the end-all, be-all cure. And when I still felt that crushing force day after day after day, for at least a few minutes or, if I was lucky enough, a few hours, my thread gave me something to grow from. It gave me something that made my pain subside.

By God's will, a short time later I was asked to visit marines at Bethesda Naval Hospital who were critically injured from the war. My only concern was screwing up in front of these dedicated individuals. As an officer and sergeant who escorted me briefed me on every marine we visited, I became more relaxed. A calming sense of a higher service took over. I became more jovial, to the point that I had to back off when one corporal who had stitches throughout the entire side of his chest asked me to stop cracking so many jokes as it made him hurt too much from laughing.

When we approached one of the last rooms, the mood suddenly changed. I was briefed about how the next marine had seen his best friend shot to death in front of him on one day, his squad leader had been killed on the following day, and the young man himself had been shot in the face two days later.

Alone, after I carefully opened the door, I walked in and maintained a genuine smile. With only one eye open due to the bandages covering half the young man's face, he held my gaze. In less than a second I felt completely ashamed of myself and all **my** worldly problems.

Sitting next to the injured marine, who was on suicide watch, was his young wife, who looked as if she had aged five years in the last five weeks; their infant son; and the man's dejected parents. Beside his lap, the young man rested his hand on his worn Bible.

Just before entering I'd been informed that late one recent evening the marine had tried to injure himself further by pulling out his various medical tubes.

As I approached the side of his bed, with every fiber of my being, I prayed for God to relieve me of my pitiful issues and instead to use me as an instrument to help ease this man's pain. I sat down on the side of the bed and grasped the marine's thick hand. Kindly, he didn't hesitate at the gesture. Since I knew he was deaf in one ear, I gently leaned over to his good ear and asked, "How we doing today?"

The young man immediately scribbled on a yellow legal pad. *Now . . . OK.*

I took in his exact words and how they related to my recent suffering and loss. I almost wanted to scoff at my own embarrassment.

All I could do was nod. Neither of us seemed to breathe or blink. I continued to hold and squeeze his hand. Silence passed between us, but we still held our stare. As my chest began to heave from shame and sorrow, I could feel the marine's body begin to shake as well. A single tear fell from his face onto the legal pad as he scribed, *? me . . . alive, every 1 else . . . gone . . . Why me?*

Inside my soul I was bare. I had nothing left. No jokes, no advice, nothing to give. I prayed to take on a moment of the marine's pain. Then, as delicately as possible, I embraced the young man, who now shook uncontrollably.

In a rare instance of grace, I whispered, "You survived for a reason. God has a plan for you. He has a plan for your boy, a boy who needs his father who will live and teach by example. I know He wants you to make your brothers proud. You've got to carry on. You've been chosen. *That's* your mission. *You're* the *one*.

"Be one of faith. Have courage and you'll get through this. As God is my witness, **you will get through this**. But now, right now, all I'm asking is for you to breathe. Draw it in, hold it, then expel it. All of it. Every single molecule. All that shit—expel it. One breath at a time, one step at a time, one day at a time. *Now*, right here right now, it's just you and I. *I need you!* Be *my* brother in arms, and together, let's . . . just . . . breathe."

I can barely remember the rest of the day or how I drove back to my hotel by the airport. In the bright clearness of the sunset I can recall that, for the first time in months, I sat straight up. I looked upwards. I called my friend George in California and said, "Today, I can breathe. If I can do that, then I believe—I know—it's going to be fine. It's going to be okay.

"It's only a divorce."

Use It or Lose It

———————◄○►———————

- Just as you have an automatic daily routine of getting dressed, getting ready for work, taking care of the kids, or having that cup of morning coffee, can you reincorporate, on a daily basis, a calming sense of belief from long ago that helped you from your past?

- Do you realize how much strength and courage it takes to open up, let in and let out feelings you may have kept buried, for whatever reason, for so long? Do you give yourself credit for even trying?

- When facing and dealing with an issue, do you believe that better days are ahead? If not, why not? If so, what is it exactly that gives you that faith?

- Can you, even though you may be beyond hurt and broken to the core, somehow step outside yourself and provide some form of comfort to others who are in more need?

- When dealing with a situation, as much as you take in all the anguish, can you process it, then, like a breath of air, expel it out, once and for all?

- Above all, do you realize you are a person of worth? That you are breathing, walking, and living on this earth for a reason? Are you willing to discover and commit to your life's mission?

CHAPTER FIVE

True Leaders?

S ometimes I just don't get it. How is it that so many folks get *so* gaga over some big-shot wanna-be, some super-ultra El Cap-i-tan of industry, armed with an endless sea of witless faces who leap—either in complete awe or in debili-tating fear—to meet his every whim, so that particular per-son can feel as if he is the supreme master of all he surveys? What's up with that?

Maybe it's just me, but I think there are a lot of folks in this vast world who get it all wrong. A lot of folks who buy into the *illusion* of who's "all that." Who's all *so* with it. Who's all *so* powerful. At some point we see "that" person during the course of our workday. That person with the deliberate "check me out" swagger, the way-too-busy, you're-so-below-me, can't-and-won't-ever-give-you-the-time-of-day attitude. Sporting the latest *GQ* or *Cosmo* over-the-top flashy clothes, barking into his or her cell phone for all to hear. Exactly three paces behind is that person's very own personal—yet terrified, naïve, just out of college, with low esteem—intern, juggling two satellite cell phones that are ringing nonstop and a telephone-book-thick legal pad, taking down whatever ramblings the Great One may spew.

Whew!

Yet at the end of the day, who really cares? Who **is** *that* person? What, if anything, has *that* person really accomplished? What has this particular individual sacrificed? What has this person endured? What lessons has this person passed on? What has this individual given to others? In a lifetime of experiences and opportunities, what exactly has this person contributed to the greater good?

Hmm?

If it's not the small-fish wanna-bes we as a society just can't seem to stop idolizing as drool seeps from our gaping mouths, then it's the over-the-top tycoon, big-city heavy hitters, the players who prey, those who make the unimaginable, unfathomable deals. We are so amazed when we see their smug mugs grinning at us with that cocky gaze on the cover of high-end big-business magazines. We race to the bookstore just to snatch up the latest, never-before-revealed secrets of the power players' *inner*, inner circle of big business. Half the readers carefully digest and dissect every word and every comma, combing for clues about how they, too, can become the next mogul (even though they do not have a single day of occupational experience). Others are giggly with amazement as the businesspeople extraordinaire brag about their exploits: the cutthroat, underhanded, ruthless techniques that took complete advantage of good, hardworking folks whose only miscalculation was that they were a little too naïve; the reality is that the corporate sharks fed off the little guy, simply because they could.

Waking Up to "Real-Life" Reality

But then, sooner or later, something happens. Something out of "their" control: world events take over, the market drops, or some small, formerly drowned-out voice with a grievance from the past bubbles up to the surface. Then the jig is up. And while some clamor for more of the show, suddenly the curtain falls. The King has not only left the building, but has fled the country with the aid of his private transport, armed only with the clothes on his back and that hidden account number to a bank in the Bahamas. There'll be no more champagne cocktails and caviar dreams with the Great Gatsby, ol' sport. And all those boastful words, all those power "techniques," are now not worth the paper they were printed on. The party is indeed over.

For every once in a while society finally gets its fill. We receive that long-overdue wakeup call. The bubble bursts—from the late 1990s high-tech, no-product, no-service, dot-com upstarts, to the recent overpriced real estate market—and reality strikes with a chilling vengeance. Even though there were those fuddy-duddy, non-flashy, unsexy, ol' folks who actually heeded warnings, who begged for caution coupled with sound practical advice, it still couldn't stop, wouldn't stop, most of the mindless herd, who, like lemmings, followed behind their newfound captains of industry to the edge—and beyond.

Why? Why do folks do this? Maybe because, in part, they believed that person had it all. That person was going places. That person was a success. That person could be trusted. *That* person was a leader. *The* leader.

Really? That's not exactly my definition of someone who motivates others through his or her actions, whether for the world to see or, more importantly, behind closed doors. I just don't seem to understand how or why some folks can be so easily swayed and taken in by these individuals, who really don't have all that much to offer.

As adults, you and I should understand the realities of the world and how certain entities operate. However, if one does business or has a relationship with a snake, one should not be surprised when—not *if* but *when*—the snake coils up, reveals its fangs, and strikes with lightning speed, releasing its toxic venom.

Personally speaking, what boils my water is those who come off as kind visionaries, caring mentors, or upstanding, leading business professionals—but are anything but. When I hear the words Enron and Tyco it just makes me fume. These executives deliberately deceived and took advantage of scores of hardworking folks—*folks they are responsible for*—knowing full well that those folks invested their life savings—*I repeat*, their *life savings*—because they believed in those who were in a position of responsibility.

And the sad part was not the tens of thousands of layoffs,

but (hang on, dear reader—I have to stop and reach over for a tissue) the crocodile tears from the wife of a top executive who spewed to the camera, "Well, what are you going to do? It's rough for everybody. I mean, we may have to sell off our fourth home and put up the Gulfstream 550 [a plush private jet] for sale until things blow over. I mean, it's hard times for us all."

Boo-hoo!

I know you know there are no guarantees in life, particularly in the stock market, but when those in a position of responsibility say, "Follow me, trust me," they should at the very least know where *they're* going. And if they get lost, when they screw up, they should be the first to take—um, what's that word? Oh yeah: **responsibility**.

Question: When was the last time you heard or learned of one of the heavy hitters, over whom so many went gaga, who got his hand caught in the cookie jar and owned up to the world? "First off, *I'm* sorry about this. I truly am. I know *I* let a lot of folks down. *I* screwed up. Yeah, it's *my* fault. And no matter what happens, *I* will try to make things right. Again, *I* am sorry and *I* beg your forgiveness."

Then there are those in corporate America who, when the going gets a wee bit too tough and events spiral out of control, reach down, grab hold of that bright red handle, and in one smooth move eject themselves from the situation. Then, while floating away, that same person watches things disintegrate, knowing all along that he has that golden parachute to ensure his own safety and needs.

Forgive me, dear reader, for you know I'm on a rant here, but as my dear friends who proudly wear the badge in the law-enforcement field preach to me, "If they buy the tickets, you're obligated to give them the full ride." I look at the whole CEO escape plan this way: Everybody takes a chance—in love, in health, in the world of business, and in just about all aspects of the virtual unknown. **We take a chance.** To me, stepping out and reaching beyond one's boundaries is what makes life all the more exhilarating. You just never know what might happen next.

In my opinion, particularly in the business world, the last great leader who truly stepped out beyond the norm, who took one hell of a chance and put others first without the aid of a golden parachute let alone a covert plan of escape, was Lee Iacocca, of the then Chrysler Corporation. He was able to turn the company around in part by applying common-sense business methods, cutting needless overhead, updating techniques and equipment, and holding firm to the ideal of better days ahead. Now, I can imagine that ol' Lee stepped on a few toes and called a spade a spade and took a few raps to the chin, but no one questioned his sincerity as a leader.

And he did all of this, if you can believe it, for the whopping salary of one dollar a year. Lee gave every ounce he had not for untold millions, but for one hundred pennies a year. Now, as an adult you can appreciate the fact that when the company turned around, Mr. Iacocca was very well compensated—as he darn well should have been—but only after those he was accountable for were taken care of first.

Let's look at the premise of that last sentence again: *compensated* for services and sacrifice. Compensated, yes; however, it was on the condition that those in his care were provided for first and foremost.

Wow! What a radical concept!

The Big "Lead"

Does any of this sound parallel to the most vital position as a leader: a parent? Do any of the preceding examples remind you of how one should act as a spouse, relative, friend, neighbor, or everyday plain John or Jane Citizen of Anywhere, USA?

Those who wish to better themselves; who live life by certain standards; who go about life—like it or not—doing what has to be done in a quiet manner, no matter the task, no matter the cost, no matter the time it takes or the odds against them; who live by example and maybe, once in a great while, lend a helping hand to others, are, in my book, *leaders*. True leaders.

Question: Are you leading by living or are you simply coasting through, collecting dust along the way?

Think about it.

"Leading by living": sounds something like a good parent to me. And that's why I go gaga over single parents. As we all know, the reality of life can be hard at times, and unfair, if not downright cold-hearted and viciously brutal.

And all the more so for the life of a single parent. Now, depending upon what you've read, heard, or observed, the average single parent is in his or her mid- to late thirties and has 1.7 kids. He or she works at *least* forty hours a week, some as much as sixty-plus, and while most have a high school diploma, the majority of these single mothers *and* fathers take in around $34,000 a year. Add to that the fact that more than half get little to no financial support from the deadbeat other parent.

Needless to say, it ain't easy.

Yet somehow, no matter what the crisis of the moment, hard times, or bad luck, they would never think of proclaiming, "Hey, everybody, I have *so* arrived—look at me!" These parents keep on keepin' on. They make things happen. They accept the situation for what it is, make the most of it, scrape by, if need be on their bloodied hands and knees, just possibly to make ends meet. And they turn things around. Why? Because, for good or ill, **that's their job!** That's their sole function. That's their life's mission!

What other option do these folks *really* have?

Obviously, single parents do not have a lot of time to loiter. They may have but a few precious moments to themselves in the wee morning hours, before the chaos ensues, or a scarce amount of time just before their head hits the pillow at the end of yet another trying day, but they really get things done. In the grand scheme of things, married parents and single parents keep the home in running order, go all out for their job at work, keep the kids safe and in check, raising them as best they can. For many, it's nothing pretty, it's nothing fancy. A bare-thread existence, but they do it. No golden parachute, no cutting corners, no scheming against others for the sole purpose of their own stellar advancement. Just stepping up to the plate day after day, after day, after day. For these good folks, bailing out when the going gets tough is not an option.

Sounds like good, wholesome, old-fashioned, true leadership to me: Living by example, being selfless and humble, with great sacrifice for others. And when one does this, whether it's for business or personal goals, suffering is just part of the crusade.

And the world is full of such stories. Academy Award winner for Best Actor in the film *Ray*, Jamie Foxx, who actually played piano for the movie, gave credit to his grandmother for helping raise him with sound moral values. "She taught me how to behave and what was expected of me. I saw how hard it was for her. It was her love and stern ways that helped keep me out of a whole lot of trouble."

Then there's another African American mother who raised three children completely by herself, never once asking for aid of any kind, *and* ensured that they all attended college, where each one graduated with honors. Two of this lady's children went on to become doctors, while the other became a prominent attorney.

The same can be said of the everyday person who goes to work at a seemingly dead-end job, with little to no advancement, and yet has no resentment while still giving it his or her all. Or that person who lives a productive life while battling a serious illness, or those who are out there right at this moment serving their country, from the entry-level private to the four-star general, "embracing the suck" (as they say) with boots on the ground, fulfilling their commitment in the war against terrorism. You lead quietly, you lead by example, you keep your chin up, and you simply do whatever has to be done!

Day by day, it may not seem like one is accomplishing a lot, or experiencing any major breakthroughs. Day by day, it may not seem like it's worth it. Day by day, you may want to pull out your hair by its roots, and scream at the top of your lungs and run into some cave and hide out forever.

In fact, it's pretty normal to think or feel like that once in a great while. That's why it's important to purge all those frustrations so they don't build up and dominate you.

However, it's the day-by-day issues that reveal to you and to others **who** you really are, what you're truly made of. When no one is watching, when you don't give a darn what others think or *don't* think about you, when you can accept the kind of person you are and what you stand for without grandstanding because you humbly believe it's the right thing to do, against insurmountable odds, **that's** the day when you have "so arrived." That's when you have become a true leader!

If any of the preceding statement resembles you in the slightest, well, you, my friend, for good or ill, big or small, are a true leader. You believe in yourself; you have a cause to pursue. And maybe you don't know it, but you probably have the genuine respect of others. At the very least, you have mine.

So take a deep breath, and, as the military would proudly state, "cowboy the hell up" and fulfill your duty. Right now the world needs and is waiting for someone just like you.

The Quiet Heroes

It was haunting as much as it was surreal. After putting in a full day at my former elementary school, I now shared a dinner with the man behind my dramatic rescue.

I nervously played with my food, barely making eye contact. I had never eaten in front of a teacher, let alone the individual who saved my life. Even though Steven Ziegler was a man, to me he was a **teacher**, my teacher. As the minutes dragged on, I noticed that he seemed a little edgy as well.

Ever since I had arrived at seven in the morning, Mr. "Z" (as I called him) kept reminding me, "I know you have a long drive back to your air force base, but there's something I really need to talk to you about." It didn't take a genius to figure out what it was. But even though I had in fact interviewed several teachers for a project that later became my first book, I didn't want to go there, especially with the man who'd seen me back in the day when I was more of an animal than a kid. The last time he had seen me, I was eating from garbage cans, smelled as if I lived in a Dumpster, and was covered with bruises on top of bruises. Now, just being in Mr. Ziegler's presence almost twenty years later as a married, young father was to me like having an audience with the Pope.

I wanted to beat him to the punch so we could just get beyond the whole thing. On the outside, I held on to an overemphasized, stupid-looking grin, while on the inside I was completely unglued.

"I, ah, I . . . just wanted to thank . . . you for all you've done for me, sir."

Just as he had when I was a twig-like child, whenever he seemed a little agitated Mr. Z sounded exactly like movie legend Clint Eastwood. "It was no big deal. All we did was call the police—they basically did the rest," he replied in a low, gravelly voice.

"But, sir, you don't understand. . . . I owe you and the others so much. You guys saved my life," I blurted out, thinking of the other teachers, the school nurse, and the principal.

"We all just did what we had to do, what should have been done," Mr. Ziegler reemphasized.

"But . . ." I continued, wanting my teacher to understand, to feel not only the severity of my situation but, more vitally, how much I felt indebted.

"No, stop. Stop it. We were only doing our job," he said with sorrow behind his words. "If anything, we should have intervened sooner." Mr. Z stopped to check himself. "The whole matter—we knew, we all knew. We had to do something. But things were different back then. The laws—there were really *no* laws back then to protect kids, let alone those reporting. Again, we just did our job. It was no big deal. Just like you did today," he said. He was referring to a scarecrow-like child who had come up to me right after school that afternoon. In a flash, from the way the anxious boy muttered, to how he kept his head bent down, to how his eyes darted around in a defensive matter, to how he fidgeted to cover his scrawny arms with his worn, thick brown jacket—even though it was too warm for one—I knew.

Having worked in juvenile hall, seeing countless kids who acted out from being abused in the worst ways, I'd learned to read the *tells*, the signs of those covering their shame and suffering. As my teacher went on about how I had assisted in an obvious situation, I raised my own hand to stop him.

"It was kinda like looking at myself, back then." I paused, reflecting on my situation. Before I became overly emotional, I shook it off. "Anyway, I just talked to the kid and turned him over to the principal. I just did what—"

"Exactly. You didn't make a big deal out of it. You just did like we did. Anyway, the year's still new. We didn't pick up on the kid. Would have, but there's just so many. You said something in your program that triggered him to seek you out. You gained his trust. He wanted help. You could have brushed him off, not taken the effort to pick up on the clues, but you showed concern, gave your time, your advice, you got him to open up and now, hopefully, he won't have to face that hell anymore. From what I understand, it's a police matter now."

All I could do was slowly nodded my head. *Yeah, today we did okay,* I quietly said to myself, passing on a prayer to the kid, whose name I suddenly could not recall.

As Mr. Ziegler and I continued to toy with our food, *he* finally released the floodgates of the needless shame he had carried over my former situation for nearly twenty years. As this seemingly hard-core, apparently disconnected figure began to open up, I accidentally dropped my fork. Even before my utensil clattered onto the dish, startling everyone around us, I instantly wept. The lead blanket–like pressure of returning to the same grounds where everything had happened was, for me, beyond overwhelming. In my own small way, aiding a boy who resembled me, seeing him sit in the same spot in the same room where I had the day I'd been taken away, was spooky. And now, as my teacher informed me about the incident that finally led him and his fellow staff members to notifying the authorities, I could no longer hold back. Part of it was the shame at how I had acted—from constantly getting in trouble for stealing food to my nauseating appearance. But, more, I wept over the small group who, at the time, had risked *so much* on my behalf. Throughout the day, I read the sorrow behind the eyes of every adult who either knew of me back in the day or was directly involved in my case. Every single one!

Craving somehow to help ease Mr. Z's suffering, I confessed, "She *was* going to kill me. Without a doubt. I always knew one day she would go too far." In the privacy of my own mind, I relived that cold, rainy Saturday when my parents separated. After dropping off a cardboard box of my father's meager belongings, Mother sped away, leaving my father standing alone in the rain. She then coldly stated that it was only a matter of time.

In a hollow, broken voice I disclosed to Mr. Ziegler, "I saw her a couple years back. I asked her if *we* could have gone too far. I remember how she suddenly stared right through me. Without any remorse, any sympathy whatsoever, she stated, 'You have to understand, David, *It* was taken away from me . . . March of '73. I was planning on disposing of *It* that summer. The only problem I had was where to hide *Its* body, David.'"

Later, outside the restaurant as we said our good-byes, Mr. Ziegler began, "When you're a teacher, as the years slide by, you have no idea . . . how these kids are going to turn out. You teach, you challenge, you guide. You just never know.

"Against all odds, you've done well. Keep challenging those kids in your programs. Tell your young boy always to apply himself in his studies. And just know we're all so proud of you, David. Keep up the good work."

When it came to my turn to say goodbye and pay homage to my savior, as much as I could usually yarn nonstop, I suddenly found myself at peace. I looked up into Mr. Ziegler's eyes and gently nodded. I am of the belief that there are times in one's life when words alone can never express the depth of one's feelings.

All I could do was take Mr. Ziegler's massive hand, shake it, and say, "Thank you. From my family to you: thank you, sir!"

In his distinctive Clint Eastwood voice, he said, "Call me Steven."

"I can never do that, sir. You're my teacher."

True Leaders?

————— ‹◦› —————

- When you see those who *act* so high and mighty, who are complete façades, how does it affect you when it comes to your set of values, your leadership capabilities?

- Can you think of any *"leaders"* who were driven by greed or fame, only to have their house of cards collapse, affecting others around them? What are you able to learn and apply from *their* experience to make *you* a better, wiser person?

- How can you best "lead by living"? How can you further harness and expand on your values?

- What is your "quiet duty" that you feel obligated to fulfill?

CHAPTER SIX

Stepping Up

Not all of us can be the President of the United States, Bill Gates, Oprah Winfrey, or Arnie Schwarzenegger. And besides the obvious financial benefits and notoriety that these folks accept with the territory, can you even begin to imagine living every day of your life, with every single thing you do (or don't do) being examined and dissected for all the world to see? Who really wants to walk a few miles in their shoes with *all* those constant burdens and endless responsibilities?

Not me.

Either way, does it really matter what others do? Does it really matter what others have, or how others choose to live their lives? Again, some people get *so* caught up in who's doing what and to whom that the more they become a voyeur—watching to watch—the more they become disconnected from their own lives and actually pursuing *their own* capabilities!

At least in the grand land of America, where opportunities are vast and dreams are surpassed, you can watch things happen, have no idea how things happen—or *you* can *make* things happen. Like the good ol' common-sense maxim states: Lead, follow, or get the hell outta the way!

I believe leadership should be calm, quiet, and by example. Leading does not have to be overwhelming. One leads in a nonpretentious manner when one simply does what has to be done. Leadership is **not** about being grandiose or about self-admiration, but rather stepping up and making that singular difference, no matter how minute or tiring the job may seem. Leadership, to me, is standing up for who you are with the commitment to follow through, whether times are fantastic or not so favorable. It's the impression one makes during one's time on this earth. To me, in a word, leadership is about one's core **values**.

As you probably already know but truly need to heed, as a leader **you** are not there to be everyone's bosom buddy. Despite what others may fantasize, leading is not a popularity contest. Question: Have you ever been at work and had a friend who's been promoted after working side by side with you, but then after a span of time your work buddy acts just a little different—a lot less horse play, far more curt, a little bit more serious? Then, as more time passes you may feel as if your coworking, beer-drinking "bud" who used to gently, politely ask, now tells you to complete a task, and your mind screams, *Well, to heck with that. Who the hell does she think she is? She's sold out. She's one of them. She's part of the system. Oh my . . . she's become "da Man"!*

Has your one-time coworker and after-hours friend truly

changed? Hell, yeah! In life, as with anything, nothing stays the same, especially in the workplace. And I know you know this—you're not stupid—but I can't begin to tell you how obtuse and how upset some folks get when others are put in a position of higher responsibility.

You've seen it and I have, too. When I was a pimple-faced teen flipping burgers and my burger bud got promoted to junior assistant manager—well, things changed. The joking and clowning around came to a screeching halt. And while Matt was still my friend after all the work was completed, when on duty, during crunch time, in the middle of a rush-hour feeding frenzy, Matt put on a different hat. As elementary as this example may be, there are some folks who don't *want* to accept the mantle of responsibility and would rather put down those who are given the opportunity. These folks may act like an immature child, saying, "Matt, I don't like you anymore—you've changed." Then, ever so slowly, life begins to pass them by. And as the young Matts of the world grow and take on more responsibility, they may turn around for a moment and say to the person who's still at the same job, with the same responsibilities, "Yes, I've changed. I'm learning, I'm growing. Why won't you?"

Lead, follow, or get the hell out of the way.

Some folks take on and accept responsibility whether it's intentional or it falls in their lap. When a parent suddenly becomes ill, a young teen may wake up one morning to discover she now has to make major decisions and spend all her free time ensuring that the family is taken care of. In the middle of World War II, then Vice-President Truman, whom many believed to be too politically weak and not strong enough to lead, surprised the world when he was abruptly summoned to the White House, only to find himself raising his right hand to take the oath as President. Afterwards, he quietly uttered, "Dear God, be with me as I take on this most awesome burden of responsibility." For some, shirking their unexpected position is not an option.

Again, no fanfare, no bells, no whistles. Just everyday, common, hardworking folks making the commitment to step up and do what has to be done. Nine times out of ten *they* are the ones out there making extraordinary changes. And in many of these unexpected situations there's little to no time. No time to cry, run, or give in. In some situations there's little to no time to think, let alone grasp the whirlwind of events. When it comes to stepping up to the plate, it can be a dramatic learning curve when everything seems to be hitting you all at once.

Over the years, I've had the extreme privilege of speaking to and getting to know thousands of humble leaders: single parents, corporate CEOs, those serving in the offices of government, law-enforcement officials of all ranges, those in the sports industry. I spent an entire day with the on-site director of the Red Cross during the recovery efforts for Hurricane Katrina. After assessing a shelter that housed thousands of families, I asked the Red Cross director the same question I had posed to all the others in his position. His response was basically the same as all those who suddenly found themselves in an overwhelming, unexpected situation, and the position of ultimate responsibility: "Even with all the years of experience, all the endless training under your belt, nothing can truly prepare you for something as massive as this."

"So what do *you* do?" I probed.

"All that I can. I have to look at what needs to be accomplished, how to fulfill the task as effectively as possible, with the best resources at our disposal."

"And when things don't go well?" I softly joked, both of us knowing full well the magnitude of the catastrophe.

"Things *never* go as planned. There is always some monkey wrench in the works. Always something you never expected. So you adapt. You keep your chin up. You keep your wits about you. You shoulder the weight and press on. You don't get distracted with minute elements that can hinder your cause. You go in knowing that some days will be better than others, and some, well . . . you just don't know if you're even moving this massive ball forward. So you have to believe in what you're doing. Not what you're *trying* to do, but what you are in fact accomplishing. Even if it's only an inch at a time, an inch a day, that's still something. It's more than you had yesterday.

"You gotta be willing to take a few hits. From all sides, all the time. It just comes with the territory. Sometimes you're all alone. Sometimes you have to keep a certain distance. Friends are friends, but we're all here committed to perform our task.

"You just do what has to be done, until the next time,

whether it's your next shift, next day, or next disaster response."

Then the gentleman gave me a wry smile and closed by stating, "And believe me, there's always a next time."

Wow. That sounds like the leadership position of a parent. For there are times when a mother, father, grand-parent, or guardian can feel like a grizzled gunnery sergeant in a combative operational area of responsibility (COAR): "Come on, let's go! Fall out. Pick up those clothes. Clean your room. Take out the kitchen trash. Complete your homework. No time for back talk. I want to see busy hands and closed mouths. Come on now. Let's get 'er done!"

Think about it. Parenthood: the never-ending frantic pace, the ear-splitting noise, finishing one engagement only to have another, more trying situation pop up, the lack of response from those you're desperately trying to communi-cate with, all while you are completely burned out and over-whelmed, knowing full well that tomorrow is indeed another day in the seemingly never-ending trench-warfare campaign of being a parent.

If you, my dear friend, are a parent—without super pow-ers or a great deal of specialized training, without a master's degree in elite managerial skills and flying by the seat of your pants and go-with-your-gut experience—you may not be certain if you're making a difference, let alone a dent. You may wonder whether those around you can hear the words coming out of your mouth, and at times you're not sure if those under your command are even alive. But hey, just like in combative operations, *never let them see you bleed*. Never let 'em smell fear. Never let 'em see you lose total control. And always let 'em think you know more than they do. Lead by example!

You're the parent, they're not, and you control the oxygen. If they sass, "Quit telling me what to do! That's not fair!" tell them, "Sweetheart, you're right, but that's the way it is." If they scream out in their know-it-all voice, "I *so* can't wait to get out of this house. You're drivin' me crazy!" stay calm. Even though they act as if they're from another solar system, *keep your cool*.

Let those around you lose control as you become even more tranquil. Why? Because you are a person of experience, you have *so* been there. You are a person of vision. You know better. So with raised eyebrows, and in a soothing but commanding tone, you reply, "Drive you crazy? Well . . . that's my job. I'm not here to be your best friend. When you have kids, then it will be your turn. Then you can drive them crazy. But for now, that's just the way it is. Now scoot!"

As a parent you are not there to be a Disneyland mom or dad. Your task is not even to raise *children* as much as it is to raise responsible, independent, productive, happy *adults*.

Whether you know it or not, like it or not, as a parent, relative, guardian, or anyone else who is associated with young ones, you are basically committed to a mission. Understand the difference?

In life, we all require the same basic leadership traits— the same discipline, responsibility, and the same steadfast determination—whether you're single or married, if you're divorced, going to college, or working one, two, or a whole string of jobs. Whether you're watching your health, your waistline, or your financial bottom line. Bit by bit, day by day, you have to stand tall. You have to remain firm in your convictions. You have to believe in the quest of your cause. You gotta go out there, at times against the wind, against whatever the hurricane throws at you, and keep chipping away.

Period.

Be Advised

To reemphasize, one does not have to be of Schwarzenegger-sized fame or behave like a self-absorbed tyrant who rules over countless folks in order to be "da Man." Make and maintain the commitment. Lead by example. Lead quietly. Simply accomplish what needs to be done.

And when you set the course plotting what you will and will not do, keep in mind that there will be some folks who will—not might, but **will**—scoff at you. Whether it's petty little sarcastic digs in front of you or far more cruel remarks behind your back, there will be those who will take immense pleasure in setting you up, and tripping you up. Pay no mind. Don't get caught up in stupid little things that in weeks, days, or even hours won't amount to squat, but can in fact distract or take away your focus.

Keep this in your back pocket: If taking the lead were easy, everyone would be doing it. The truth of the matter is that, whatever their reason or excuse, there are just some folks who can't or won't step up. Whether they are couch potatoes or have quietly given up on themselves, these folks have decided to call it a day or maybe have never tried. As you know, some may carry deep resentment. The more *you* go for it, the more *you* succeed, the more inferior *they* may feel. There are also individuals who feed off a dramatic life of woe-is-me, never-ending misery. Like crabs trying to crawl out of a bucket, these folks automatically reach up, latching on to anyone, fighting to make it out of their pit of despair.

I'm not disrespecting anyone, for there are many good folks who live life on the sidelines. Not all of us can be the Super Bowl quarterback 24/7. I'm only trying to inform you that the more you strive to achieve, the more you set the pace, the more entangled and the more political things can become.

Whether it's in-laws or other relatives, those at work, the small army of kids with different needs and different maturity levels, or community commitments, you will in fact ruffle a few feathers. That's something you just have to accept.

The Big Picture

That's why you have to have a vision—*you* conceive it, *you* nurture it, and *you* strive to see it through. No matter how overwhelming things may be, you hold fast. No matter what others may say or do, no matter the doubt, you have to know in your heart what is true and why you do what you do. And that should be enough. As a spiritual man, I believe that if your higher power is for you, who or what can ever be against you?

Like our courageous men *and* women of the Vietnam War would always tell each other when situations became ugly, "Keep the faith, brothers and sisters. Keep the faith!"

Even if you're standing all alone in a vast field of debris that stretches as far as the eye can take in with unimaginable chaos and human suffering the likes of which have never been seen, if all you can do is make an inch of progress, if that's the best you can do, then accept the fact that at least you're there, that **you are** making a difference. With rolled-up sleeves, shove your critics aside and just believe you are in fact doing what needs to be done. No praise, no red carpet, just a vision and a good heart.

And that should be enough.

Stepping Out and Stepping Up

I had it all and even more than I ever imagined. I was in my mid-twenties, married, had a little boy whom I totally adored, and actually got paid for the most amazing job ever conceived: mid-air refueling for the United States Air Force's SR-71 Blackbird.

No humdrum, nine-to-five, rat-race life for me. No way! I was tasked to fly at various times of the day as needed, and every flight or mission was for me a whirl-wind, amazing adventure.

For me, even going to work was cool. I'd suit up in my Nomex, one-piece, green flight suit, don my red-and-white-checkered scarf, kiss the wife, hug the kid, and drive to the base's flight line in my compact SUV, taking in the fresh air while listening to my favorite song on my high-end cassette player.

I truly lived in the best of both worlds. I had a loving family who were safe and well provided for at home, and my other family was my flight crew, which con-sisted of the aircraft commander, a younger copilot, a navigator, and myself, a boom operator. Like all tight crews, we were basically inseparable. We spent hours planning the most minute aspects of every sortie, from when to flip a certain switch to what was required of us in the event of a catastrophic emergency. The "same crew" mentality was inherent in the nature of flying: the bonds of trust would save not only crucial seconds, but, in the event of an unforeseen event, also the lives of more than just an aircraft flight crew.

Having survived my childhood, working my tail to the bone while trying to fit in as a foster child, and then feeling humiliated as a cook in the swamps of Florida, now, with a few years under my belt as a certi-fied combat aircrew member and the internal demons put to pasture, I had *finally* begun to feel comfortable in my own skin.

Every time I'd return from an exhausting flight back to base housing, I'd sit on my front-yard swing replay-ing the events of my mission and praising God for granting me all of my blessings. I loved nothing more than watching my preschool boy rip down the street on his bright red bike with training wheels, or seeing him playing with the army of other neighborhood kids on our yard's Slip 'N Slide, or, in our private moments, playing a game of baseball with him.

At the end of the long day, after reading and then tucking Stephen into bed, I'd flop down in front of the TV, where I flipped through the channels at hypersonic speed. When I scanned through the news I'd see how parts of Los Angeles were more like a Middle East war zone due to the drugs coupled with the gang-on-gang violence. Like most folks, I'd gaze at the carnage and catch the sound bite before zoning out until the next dramatic story, or simply flip to another, less threatening channel. On a rare occasion, when channel surfing through the national news, I'd see a story about how a child was locked in a birdcage of a basement, or a young girl was prostituted by her stepfather, or how three siblings were jailed in a nearby barn for years and the neighbors had no idea that they even existed. For the most part, when I saw the results of the graphic drive-by shootings and the lost faces of innocent children, as much as I gave out a quick prayer, I was more selfish, thanking God Almighty that "those things" didn't happen here.

When I first heard it, the echo, the distinctive sound that rang from across the street, I knew. The shouts from the enraged mother. The putrid, hate-filled language that spewed from her onto her preschool-aged daughter, who sometimes played with my boy. Then the slaps. Followed by the screams—not the whimper-like cry after falling down or even from a toddler who didn't want to go to bed—but the screams that made one's skin crawl. Finally, the pitch of the terror was instantly cut off, as if someone were cupping the little girl's mouth. In my mind, as I had when I lived in the basement, I flipped the switch. I switched back to "combat protective" mode.

For more nights than I can remember, Patsy and

I talked about the little girl. We both agreed that the mother was abusive. Patsy dismissed it to the pressure of being an unfulfilled military dependent who was just "a loud person." I too found myself brushing off the latest episode, as I was soon due to deploy overseas to Asia for well over a month. But even while on my operational deployment, whenever Patsy and I spoke, we always touched on the happenings with that little girl.

For years I had done all that I could to keep my darkness at bay. I had, in fact, *lied* about my past when I was interviewed for my high-level security clearance. I had willfully committed perjury. When asked about my childhood, I soft-shoed the answer, stating, for the record, that everything had basically been normal, that "I just didn't . . . quite *get along* with my mother."

I was fully aware that my deceit was intentional. That if exposed, if proven, my falsification would not only strip me of my precious aircrew wings, but I would also be punishable under the United States Code of Military Justice. I knew what I was doing. I more than took the chance. I preferred to take the risk of hiding than to be taken off flight status for an extensive "psych eval" and open the lock box to my past.

As time wore on, it became a hard balancing act.

At home, I could mow the grass, wash the SUV, flip through any TV channel, budget the finances, and dedicate time to my family. At work, I had absolute command and control over six to eight separate aircraft within a certain amount of airspace at a given time. Through my skills, training, and passion I could make the surgical air-to-air "contact" with my refueling boom, which was extremely dangerous, look like an aeronautical ballet.

With every ounce of my being, I wanted to keep Pandora's box locked away in the deepest depths of the ocean, but somehow I knew I couldn't. Eventually my eyes, my ears, and my heart opened to all that had always swirled around me. One night while on my knees, with Stephen sleeping peacefully in his bed, I sought guidance. Within a short span of time, it came to me through a string of consecutive events: hearing of a father who murdered then quickly buried his boy only to be captured years later, who, during the sentencing phase, whimpered to the court that he had to use drugs and discipline his child because he, too, was a victim of child abuse; learning of other bizarre nationalized cases; and knowing what happened in my neighborhood just across the street. As a matter of morality, it all became inescapable.

In part because of my childhood and also due to my military experiences where I saw the lives of those from other countries and how they functioned, I wholeheartedly believed in the spirit of the American dream: the opportunity to better oneself and overcome any obstacle, to be free of oppression and live the life that any individual chooses for him- or herself.

I was extremely proud of my career. As minute as my part was in the overall grand scheme of things, through my dedicated, patriotic efforts, due to my actions and the seriousness of my oath of enlistment, I contributed to the protection and preservation of my country. Yet at a more direct level, I did nothing. I chose to do absolutely nothing for those within my grasp who truly needed a helping hand.

While I knew that people held candlelight vigils followed by marching in song to the capitol steps to "take back the night" one evening a year, as dramatic and heartfelt as that was, I now felt compelled to make an impact that was somehow more concrete.

But I had absolutely no idea what I could offer. I didn't have one of my typical Pelzer-patient, anal-retentive "master plans." I had no plan at all. If anything, I followed my heart. I felt that, with my past and my drive, I could help so much more than strolling in the evening with strangers so I could rant and rave about the horrors of injustice while toting a candle. So I went to every agency within the twin counties, asking, then pleading, to assist directly at any level. Eventually, but only after proving myself to the hilt, did my persistence pay off. After a fair amount of training and getting to know the personnel of various departments, I went from being a Youth Service worker to serving at the local juvenile hall. Over time, I branched out from volunteering for several foster-care and child-abuse-prevention agencies as well as prisons, to giving lectures at colleges throughout the state on how those who may have suffered at a young age can and should overcome and reclaim their lives.

Within two years I had gone from solely maintaining a rigorous flight schedule that kept me out of the country six to nine months a year to now incorporating not only a work schedule at juvenile hall but a calendar filled with endless volunteer appearances. I got to the point where I would schedule my precious military leave just so I could drive nine hours one way to volunteer even more.

The further I became involved, the more I learned how rampant child abuse and its collateral afteraffects are. I began to feel I couldn't do enough. At the end of one of my air force flights I could have a beer or a Coke and laugh with my crew. At home I could play ball with my son and share a lovely dinner with my family. Yet once being reexposed to the darkness, in the back of my mind, when I felt at ease, a wet blanket of guilt would wrap around me. I began to feel miserable that while I was safe and sound, there were so many who at that same moment endured unmentionable suffering.

Between Patsy, my son Stephen, my air force family, and my campaign, even though it was all my doing, I felt pulled in every direction. Then on top of it all, with all that I did, over time, it garnered unwanted recognition: a commendation from President Bush Sr., a private visit with former President Reagan, as well a Volunteer of the Year award.

As much as I had opened up to Patsy, I felt too ashamed to let her in, to truly inform her why I was so dedicated. As for the air force, with every day my fear of being exposed weighed more heavily.

I never saw it coming. And if I did, I was too absorbed to really pay that much attention. By the time I was in my early thirties, I was out of the air force, still doing part-time "pickup" shifts at the same juvenile hall, and, to make ends meet, I hand-sanded kitchen-cabinet doors for five dollars an hour. Even with our finances strained to the limit, I still felt the need to volunteer as much as I could. In the end, in part because of all that I did for total strangers while not being there all the time for my own family, Patsy and I divorced.

I moved away and into a single-room summer cabin that was older than I by at least two decades, and one day found myself sitting outside on the steps of a deck, shivering to the bone beneath the towering redwood trees. In the middle of my first winter, I pondered my past and a certain bleak future. Even after being presented with the prestigious Outstanding Young Person of the World award just weeks ago, I was destitute and felt unworthy in more ways than I could count.

Since I was a child, I had pushed myself in any way possible in part to stay away from the darkness. As a young adult, I continued the pattern, only with far more intensity. My focus had always been an honest effort to improve myself. I didn't want to become swallowed by my past, as I had seen happen firsthand to so many others. But once I knew in my heart that so many were suffering, I could no longer stand by idly and do nothing. I believed that after enduring all that I had, for me to remain passive was the worst thing I could do.

So as I sat on the dampened wooden steps with the rain seeping through my clothes, I prayed for those I longed to be with. I gave thanks for at least having a roof to provide me shelter and an air mattress to lie on. I had more than others. As pitiful as I felt and as alone as I was, I was grateful that at the very least, for a period of my life I had more than anyone could have ever dreamed of.

As I stood up and shook off the blanket of wetness, I prayed for guidance. That above all, after what I had been through and after all that I had tried to do, there had to have been a reason. That it was all part of some master plan.

Closing the door behind me as I entered the cabin, I prayed for a sign.

Stepping Up

———◄○►———

- In the age of "ant-under-a-microscope" instantaneous, non-stop news, do you feel that your efforts need public recognition to encourage you to continue? Do you find yourself wondering if you're really making a difference if no one ever acknowledges what you do? Or do you prefer to work quietly in the background and feel you are more willing not only to undertake a project but also to follow through with it to the end if you don't ever have to be in the spotlight?

- Whether in the personal or business aspects of your life, do you see yourself more as the person who has to take charge, who has to be the responsible one?

- Do you find yourself adrift, more of a person who "goes along" with the crowd? If so, do you do this in part because it makes you feel safe? Is part of it because you're afraid to step out of your comfort zone?

- Are you the type who would rather just be alone and keep the covers over your head as the world goes by?

- When did you become aware of the traits above? Is one of them more dominant than the others? If so, can you adjust in order to make your life more balanced?

- From deep within, behind all the smiles and pretense that others may flash your way, do you realize that there are certain individuals who do not have your best interest in mind? Will coming to terms with that deter you? If so, how much?

- Knowing that others may actually be against you, how far are you truly willing to take your mission?

- For those achievements you've already completed, with time to look back objectively, was it worth all the time, energy, lost opportunities, and moments in life that can never be recaptured?

- While still achieving the outcome you desire, what would be the one thing you could have done differently? How will that affect you in your next endeavor?

- No matter the price paid or the outcome of your efforts, can you at least give yourself some credit for stepping out and stepping up?

CHAPTER SEVEN

The True Mentor

Visualize, if you will, the cramped, oven-like cockpit of a United States Air Force refueling tanker, flying an approach for a practice landing.

"Tanker, turn onto heading two, niner, zero," a voice instructs.

"Roger, air traffic control, turning onto two, niner, zero."

"Co, this is pilot—watch altitude—you're a little low."

"Pilot, Co, copy. Increasing altitude. Coming up."

"Co," I say, sitting behind and in between the pilot and copilot in what is called the jump seat, "you're a little slow—increase power. . . ."

"Boom, I copy. Increasing."

"Air force tanker, air force tanker, be advised your heading is now three, one, zero approaching three, two, zero correct heading, turn left, turn left **now**."

"Co, lower landing gear," commands the pilot.

"Co," I pile on, "lower flaps to thirty. Check forward tank fuel pumps. Check airspeed."

"Watch your bank angle!" the pilot advises, raising his voice.

"Roger, I copy," you, as the copilot, huff as you wipe the beads of sweat dripping from your tired eyes. "I'm on it. I'm on it. Gear, coming down. Fuel pumps turned . . . on . . . increasing airspeed . . . increasing altitude . . . turning **to** heading three, two, zero—"

Then without warning, the cockpit fills with a single word—from the pilot, the aircraft's navigator, and myself: "Abort!" A split second later air traffic control commands, "Air force tanker, abort your approach. Abort. Go around. Go around."

Suddenly the instructor pilot takes over, instantly levels the wings, applies proper rudder control and slips the wallowing aircraft onto a proper heading, adjusts airspeed, and readjusts the flaps. All in a matter of two, three seconds tops, as if he were flicking a fly off his shoulder. Then, in a mock disgruntled voice, the veteran aviator leans over to you, the twenty-three-year-old, wet-behind-the-ears copilot, and sneers, "What in the hell are **you** doing? Are **you** flying this jet or is this jet *flying* **you**?"

Now, dear reader, stay in the zone for a moment longer and imagine all that high-pitched noise filling your headset, which has two different radios constantly yelling curt commands at you from different agencies at the same time, plus three other members from your crew watching, dissecting, advising, then telling you not only what to do, but when and how to accomplish your task. Your one hand is trying to steer the aircraft while the other fumbles through an endless array of switches and fuel throttles, and all while your eyes strain to stay focused on the inside of the cockpit and the outside runway environment.

On top of all that you're basically a kid—with a little acne still on your chin, maybe a year into your air force service commitment, which means you're just out of college—and now you're overwhelmed with attempting to jostle a mammoth piece of metal that has been flying since thirty years *before* you were born, carrying 70,000 to 80,000-plus pounds of highly volatile fuel. And this is the last hour of your day that began ten hours before.

Hoo-wee!

Taking control or even just trying to manage life—love, family, friends, work, home, health, and whatever else comes your way. Wow! Intense. Overwhelming. To some, utterly, completely, unmanageable. But God bless those who step into the breach or strap themselves into the seat of something bigger than themselves. Bless those who at least give it a shot.

Now I can understand that some of you may be thinking the preceding is just a twisted, macho, over-the-top aircrew-member ritual. Absolutely not! Nothing would be further from the truth. The example is really a lesson in management. Management of one's time, one's focus, and one's resources. It's learning how to conduct, and when to regulate, a sequence in the performance of one's task. A valuable lesson in getting behind and aiming the eight ball of life.

Think about it.

Remember this: *You cannot lead if you cannot manage.*

Whether in sunny skies or gale-force winds, you plot your destination, maintain your course, and hold fast to your convictions. In life you're either manning the helm or you're just unmarked cargo used for ballast, dead weight.

So here's a question: In **your** life, right now, in real-time reality, are you flying your jet? Are you the captain of your ship, or are you stumbling around in a stupor? Are you just a lifeless passenger, a blind-to-the-world-around-you observer, being tossed from side to side like a worn rag doll?

I certainly hope not.

With all my heart, I am of the belief that nearly all folks simply wish to live their lives in their own way, doing their own thing, for their own reasons. And for the most part, I've found that folks wish to do better. To better themselves and their surroundings. In all honesty, I can't say that I've met too many people who have run up to me saying how much they wish for, how much they crave, someone or something that would dictate their lives for them.

Choosing for yourself, living as you wish, kind of sounds like freedom to me. What do you think?

Manage the small, seemingly insignificant things in order to direct more important matters of life. It's not going to happen overnight, but if you're consistent, it will happen. Learn to walk before you attempt your marathon race.

Yet what gives me pause, what causes me duress, at times bordering on intense apprehension that makes me want to pull out my hair, is that there are some who have lived their lives for many, many, many years with not a hint of ambition.

These folks have no goals to better themselves or their surroundings, let alone helping out and lending a hand to others. They have made any and every excuse, have calculated, sometimes with savage malice, every angle to their selfish indulgence, while pointing the finger of blame at others. In reality, through their own decisions, their own actions *and/or* inactions, they failed to step up. Yet lo and behold, suddenly, with passion and vigor, they become the one and only know-it-all, whizbang *expert* on a subject. These types of individuals suddenly have vast knowledge and practically demand that you, dear reader, instantly listen and heed their mighty words about how you should now live your life!

What in heaven's name is that all about? Maybe I'm off my rocker, but to me that's not even close to sound leadership, management, or even ownership.

I'm in no way going out of my way to be callous, but I personally know an individual we'll call E.M. who has conned, lied, and cheated everyone at all levels—from family members, including an elderly grandparent and a mentally disabled sibling, to friends, business associates, you name it. E.M. was dishonorably kicked out the armed forces within weeks of enlistment, had various lawsuits and DUIs, and filed bankruptcy protection even against the grandparent who *loaned* E.M. the money to file the bankruptcy paperwork in the first place.

E.M. is blatantly jealous of others who have not only come to terms with their issues, but after years of grueling work and sacrifice, who are also now content in their lives.

E.M. feels "left behind," just a mere two steps behind everyone else. If that weren't enough, E.M.'s attitude is arrogant beyond words. If anyone mentions past transgressions, the lightning response is, " 'F' 'em. It's my way or the highway." E.M. lives for attention, inventing over-the-top scenarios with, of course, E.M. right in the middle of all the high-end drama—from the death of family members, to nearly being a victim of the 9/11 aircraft hijackings. E.M. later boasted that this avoidance of harm was a result of personal "premonitions."

(Thank the Lord!)

E.M. justifies the drinking, the drugs, the cons, and the swath of destruction by having a dark past. Most of that *really* bothers me. None of us is perfect; all of us have something in our pasts that we're not all too proud of. But what sickens me is when someone like E.M. suddenly, without remorse, without making amends, without helping others, without any training, *decides* to become the master, super-duper entity for all to hear and take heed of.

Maybe you've encountered an E.M. in your life. A person who, instead of striving to improve a negative situation, uses it as an excuse not only to dwell in the misery, but also to further enhance that misery with self-destructive behavior. These types of people seem to feel society *owes* them because they suffered. They may even resent you, either because they don't think you've suffered as they have or because they can't get beyond their own situation as you are trying to do—they embody that old saying: misery loves company.

When I was finally able to crack through a few thick layers of E.M.'s defensive ego during one of many phone calls, the response I received was, "You were lucky, David. You were removed. I was never taken away. *You* have no idea what it was like."

Okay, I said to myself, keeping my mouth shut. Now, I wouldn't say I was lucky to be subjected to my past. However, to be honest, it was horrible that while I was taken away and placed in the bosom of social services, there was nothing done to save or protect my four other brothers who had to deal with my mother's wrath. That in itself has constantly haunted me for a majority of my life.

"What happened?" I probed. "Please tell me. I really want to understand."

"You think . . . you think you were the only one?" E.M. choked up, as if tears would spill at any second.

"Please," I genuinely pleaded, "tell me. Was it physical? Were you beaten?"

"Huh?"

"*Your* abuse. Were you tortured? Were you constantly beaten? Were you starved?" I asked, throwing out any example I could, hoping to stimulate any type of response.

"Uh . . . no. No. Of course not."

"*Okay*," I continued. "Were you ever sexually abused, raped, sodomized, molested, touched—anything of this nature?"

"No!" E.M. immediately barked in a resentful tone.

"Well," I returned, "what the hell did happen?"

After a few seconds, E.M. let out a deep breath. That's

when I felt we were near a breakthrough. *Thank God*, I thought, *now E.M. can begin to come to terms.* "I got yelled at. All the time. I mean all the time. I was slapped. I was told I was stupid. I was ugly, that my red hair was disgusting. I was chased around the house. I was threatened. But then I'd chase back. I was made to feel inferior. I was made to think I wasn't smart, that I wasn't pretty."

Pretty? I thought to myself as I continued to pay close attention to the voice on the other end of the phone.

At the end of the long, dragged-out, mind-numbing conversation, I so wanted to believe I had made a chink in this individual's defensive armor. At least that was a start. To me, it in no way justified E.M.'s misdeeds or continued actions or superior attitude, but now I had something to connect the dots with regarding why this individual craved so much attention.

I knew E.M. had in fact been physically and psychologically abused. There was no doubt about that. But while E.M.'s siblings adopted a more honorable, challenging path of hard work and true-grit determination, E.M. copped out, cheating in any way possible, *choosing* a different trail. Plain and simple.

Whew. I gotta take a breath here.

I believe there is not one of us on this planet who hasn't been affected by some horrible, undeserved situation. Hopefully, we learn, we grow, we turn things around, we make things better. To me, that's leadership: setting the bar from good solid experience and by sound example. What I cannot tolerate is a person who suddenly believes he deserves to take the helm for the sole purpose of bathing in the spotlight of recognition because as a pre-teenager, this person's perpetrator made *him* feel inferior and made him think *he* was not pretty.

And yes, dear reader, this middle-aged *man* blames others for the outcome of his life because he has always wanted nothing more than to be superior and admired by others. To this day, *he* is adamant about *not* making any gesture of apology or atonement, yet still wants, craves, and demands respect from others, believing he is a person who is *so* qualified to lead.

Personally speaking, I think it's nothing short of sickening.

Now hold on, dear reader—please don't think I'm hitting below the belt. The preceding example gives me absolutely no pleasure, but I have personally known of this person's road of destruction for more than half of my life. And with all of my heart I hope and pray for this man to come to terms, grow the hell up, and truly become a sound, contributing member of society.

Regardless, I am of the firm stance that one should walk the walk for many, many, many untold, unknown, unadvertised miles before one even thinks about informing others about how to tie their shoes.

As a person who works hard, as a person who at least tries to make improvements, the question I pose to you, dear reader, is: *What do* **you** *think*?

Having an idea is one thing. Wanting to do something

for others is nice. Cleaning up from past episodes is indeed another fine gesture. And they are all worthy and deserving of respect, if one's intentions are true. But to assist and to lead takes time. It takes true heartfelt commitment, *all the time*. Setting the pace is basically the manner in which we live our lives.

The challenges of life and time will test your mettle. Maybe to see in some strange way if you are indeed worthy of the cause.

I'm not trying to pull the rug out from under anybody, but to be a parent, to manage a team in business, to stand up to an injustice, or to hold yourself to a standard takes a lot more responsibility and exertion than some are willing to practice. For there are those who only want to take over the *Good Ship of Hope* and command the helm under clear blue skies and on smooth-as-glass seas, rather than pilot the craft in rough, white-capped waters.

Which poses the obvious question: Are you ready for this? Are you up to the challenge, the loneliness, the heartache, the scoffing from others, the disappointment and untold suffering that only you and God will realize? Can you, will you, stand tall against the storm of despair when things aren't so smooth?

There are some people who make things look easy. Mr. Tiger Woods comes to mind. "Wow, it must be *so* hard being out there playing golf all day for a living," some may scoff sarcastically. I say, well then go out there and do it yourself. Let's not forget that in reality this man has been out there putting and driving that little white ball since before kindergarten *every day*. Now let's not forget that his father, Earl, wasn't even allowed to step foot on some of those golf courses because, *oh my God*, Earl Woods (who was good enough to serve his country as an officer in the United States Air Force) was black. But hey, after years and years of steadfast commitment and untold sacrifices, Tiger makes it all look so easy, as a true leader in the game. He is an immense inspiration to millions of folks of all ages **and** races, whether they whack that little white ball or not.

Another name that pops into mind when it comes to true-grit, how-do-you-like-those-apples, bring-it-on determination is Lance Armstrong. Ol' Lance literally rode the comeback trail of battling cancer and a grueling career as a bicyclist but didn't get all that much attention until after he won his fourth—I repeat, fourth—back-to-back Le Tour de France.

To me, just as important to society is that sweet married couple down the street and that single parent with the nice, well-behaved teenage kids. No one sees the time, the tears, the frustration, the resolve, the boatload of drudgery it took behind the scenes just to keep the union together, or to keep little Joey off the street and his sister Michelle away from drugs. Again, for those lazily coaching from the sidelines, I'm sure it all looks easy.

And that's in part what good mentors do. They make it appear simple, keeping it simple while living life simply.

I know you know this. All of this. You and I are not children, but having a true deep respect and appreciation for a cause, your cause, is another thing entirely. Few of us, *especially* me, are qualified to land a wallowing jet that takes out an entire city with its load of volatile fuel that is just seconds away from tumbling out of control. But God love and God bless the person who truly straps in, who has truly studied, who certifiably passed every challenge and **still** fights to take on all that can be thrown at him. At the end of the day, if you can walk away from a bumpy landing, a not-so-good day at work, or a trying time with the family, well, I hope you can draw a positive experience from it, and make taking on that approach vector another day easier.

If this is you, good luck. Study up, buckle in, sit up, and pay close attention to your checklist and your personal moral compass. You're cleared for approach, so lower, and check, *and* recheck your gear. Verify your flaps, maintain your current heading, and keep your eyes on your inside and outside environment.

And, of course, enjoy the ride.

It's Always Something

"No way!" I huffed as I ran through the Denver airport, frantic to make my next series of back-to-back flights. "You have got to be kiddin'. That's a good one. For a moment you had me. You sounded serious."

A few seconds later I came to a sudden stop as hundreds of people rushed around me. "No, Dave," Chrissy, my editor, gently inserted, "there's been a mistake and we need to add more to the book."

Still not taking it all in, I asked, "You're serious?" for the tenth time in less than a minute.

"I'm afraid so." Chrissy exhaled. "I just found out myself. I know it's a big deal—I know how busy you are—but we've got to do this. I'm sorry, I truly am, but . . ."

I could feel a sudden crushing weight bear down on me. As much as I tried, I couldn't shake it off. I shook my head from side to side before sprinting through the terminal to make my next flight. "No!" I announced. "I can't do it."

"Dave, you've got to understand, this has no bearing on your writing. The book is solid, it's just—"

Now running at full speed, weaving among herds

of people sauntering too slowly for my taste, I barked back, surprising myself as I could feel the tension from within me rising, "No way. You and I finished, what—a week, two weeks ago? You said it was a wrap. No. I'm done with it, the whole thing."

I was in no way trying to be arrogant or rude. I despised that in people, especially those "one-week wonder" bestsellers who ran down those in the business who took a chance and made them who they were. As an editor, Chrissy was more than kind and patient with my quirky personality and my high-speed lifestyle. When it came to the line-by-line editing of the manuscript, which I dreaded more than the writing even though I was anal with the pacing, the exact wording, and every example given in my works, Chrissy made the entire process non-threatening and easy to accomplish. After countless hours on the phone, Chrissy seemed more like a kid sister to me. I respected and admired her immensely.

But now I felt threatened. What she did not know, what I had not revealed to her but instead to only a handful of senior staff members of my team, was that the latest manuscript was the hardest project I had ever attempted. With it, I had stepped way beyond my comfort zone. I had been married to the project for well over four years, and during that time I went through a heart-wrenching divorce, assisted in cleaning up after the devastation of Katrina, became even

more involved with the military—including traveling
to Iraq—and, in between everything else, I had re-
started my degree in criminal justice, was in produc-
tion of my next tome, and had just signed on to host a
major radio show. All in all, I just wanted to be done
with that book.

"Chrissy, you don't understand!" I again shook
my head while my brain cascaded down over its endless list. "No way. I can't do it. My life—everything
I do—is planned, to even when and how long I can
steal a nap. I would have never signed on for the radio
show, volunteered to work with the military—It's all
too much as it is. I don't have the time. I've got nothing
else to give. I'm spent. Please, don't make me do this.
Listen, I gotta go," I ended, zipping through the jet way
as I boarded the airplane.

As embarrassed as I was at having ended the conversation in an unmannerly way, within seconds I was
back on the cell phone bitterly complaining to my liter-
ary agent and my office's executive director, trying to
find a way to avoid the challenge.

It took a couple of days for me to cool down. Only
then was I able to take it all in. Even when Chrissy first
broke the news to me at Denver International, I knew I
would have to "cowboy up." Part of my resistance was
that it takes me so long to scribe a single paragraph.
After numerous phone calls, when everyone finally
got together, we laid out a plan. It was simple: I would

literally devote every free second I had to work on the book.

After a few chapters, I found my groove. The less pressure I put on myself, the less I resisted, the more things seemed to flow from me. Due to my extensive appearances that were scheduled months before, I had to adapt to little or no sleep for days at a stretch. I really didn't mind. With so many people and so much involved with the book, I switched from wanting to be done with the project to recommitting to making the tome the absolute best that I could. I could accept nothing less. That in itself gave me solace. There were days when I was more of a zombie than a human being, like when I worked through three straight shifts camped out at a local Starbucks. Like everyone else who faces a challenge, I kept telling myself, *I'll do what I have to do.*

For me, it was only when I accepted my fate that I seemed to open up, giving more than I ever thought possible.

At the end of each chapter, before e-mailing the new sections to Chrissy, my executive director, Mrs. "C," would review the additions. Mrs. C, a very spiritual woman, always gave me a courtesy nod. At times, after reading a few pages, she would wipe the tears away with a tissue.

"This was meant to happen. God wanted you to do this. This is going to help out so many people. Just like your speaking and your radio show, it's all about telling your story. I know you're beyond that. But for now, God wants you to do this. Look at all the signs. It's all clicking together."

Remembering her words late one night after finishing another section, I smoked my celebratory cigar. As my emotions began to settle after writing, I exhaled slowly. I had at least a few hours off. I had a few hours to clear my head and count my blessings.

Whenever I faced a challenge, especially the unexpected and overwhelming ones, I always seemed to reflect on where I came from and how fortunate my life has truly become. I could think of no other person who was as lucky as myself. Even with all the chaos, the wild rollercoaster-like highs and lows, and the absolute, petty, needless bullshit flung my way, at least my life was an adventure. At least I had a purpose. Even if I failed, at least I tried.

For me, all good things seem to evolve when I least expect them. That night, without thinking, as always, at the end of a long day, I made the sign of the cross across my chest. However, that evening I vowed, "I'm not going to fight it. Do with me as you wish. I know I can do better. I know I can be better. I'm ready to listen. I'm ready to accept my fate."

The True Mentor

————◦————

- At times when elements of your life seem to take over, what do you do (or can you do) to keep from being overwhelmed?

- When you become overtaken, do you shut down, do you resist, or do you lash out against others? How long and how strong is your initial reaction? How long does it take you to accept an unfortunate situation?

- What makes you feel secure, helps you face the situation and begin to turn things around?

- How does it make you feel to see someone you know seem to get away with so much while you continue to strive to better yourself or those around you? Does it distract you at times? If so, do you realize how much time and energy it takes away from your focus?

- Even when it may seem as if there is no light at the end of your endeavor while those around you are in fact complete façades and morally bankrupt, do you take pride in simply being true to yourself and your cause?

CHAPTER EIGHT

Holding the Line

Recently I read *and* heard a few hard-to-believe, over-the-top stories about a particular father who seemed like a cold, heartless barbarian. Supposedly this fellow would march throughout the house, constantly tripping over his kids' various toys. As time went on, he would warn the kids about putting their belongings in their proper places—*or else*. Then one day one of the kids exclaimed, "Daddy! Daddy! Where's my toy?" The father leaned over and in a curt voice stated, "I took it. It's gone."

Now, can you imagine the little tyke bursting into tears while jumping up and down, stomping his feet, "That's . . . that's not fair. How could you? You . . . you meanie. It's mine. Mine! Mine! Mine!" Then after the volcanic temper tantrum passed, the father again bent forward and in a calm tone warned, "*Now* . . . go pick up the rest of your toys."

Wow!

This same fellow, after warning the kiddies about turning off their bedroom lights when not in their rooms, would later go in and take out all the bulbs if the tykes did not obey. One time I heard an outrageous tale in which his daughter left her dress on the floor. Rather than picking it up and putting it away for her, the father supposedly tossed the garment into the fireplace.

Wow again!

Now, whatever you think of how he handled those situations, this fellow makes a point. He takes a position, states his purpose, and holds his ground.

And, like all parents, he sat down and explained his actions to his children: that he is an immigrant to this nation; that he came from post–World War II Europe, born and raised in Austria where times were hard at best. Where opportunities were less than limited. How hardworking, good folks could not fulfill their greatness because of Communist strife. So he took a chance. He dreamed, and longed for America. When he arrived he worked hard. *Very, very, very hard.* He sacrificed. He endured, then endured even more. He earned his luck and worked harder still. Always striving, always reaching, always expanding his boundaries. This individual saw firsthand a portion of naturalized Americans who seemed to be stagnant in their lives, complaining, wishing, wanting, crying, craving for things to get better, moaning about how times were so hard, so bad. But this fellow *at least* went out and *did something*, accomplishing more than many in this nation could even fantasize about.

At the end of this *barbaric* father's epic story, one can imagine him pointing a finger in the children's direction and purposely stating, "Just because your last name is Schwarzenegger doesn't mean you get a free ride in life. Cah-lee-for-nia is in an energy crisis, so mind the electricity. Money, toys, clothes, this nice home are all from the yield of what your mother and I worked hard for. You all must learn respect. Learn to appreciate all that we have. One day soon you will have to go out on your own and make your way."

Again, at the very least we know where Ol' Arnie stands.

And while some may scoff and say, "Well, that's just another Hollywood megalomaniac trying to fill his inflated ego," I don't agree. He's not alone in his stance. I know of a lady who as a child was constantly told and warned, then berated about the disarrayed state of her room. Then, one day, out of the blue, oh my gosh, the young girl came home, scampered up the stairs, and bounced happily into her room, only to discover in horror that her favorite little doll had disappeared. So she tore apart her room, searching high and low, and scoured every nook and cranny, but still no pretty little dolly-doll.

"Did you ever find it?" I asked my friend.

"No," she responded. "But when I went to ask my mom what happened, I immediately knew. She sat me down and kindly but firmly explained why she had taken away my favorite doll."

"What did you do? How did you feel?"

"Man, was I pissed! That was *my* doll and that was *my*

room. What could I do? Well, after I whined to no avail, as all young kids do, I marched back upstairs, put my room together, and never—and I mean never—disrespected my mother's warnings ever again. I kept that room tight. Nothing was ever out of place."

This lady worked with me as a counselor in juvenile hall, so I asked her what effect that one seemingly insignificant event may have had on her life. Her face changed. "That one incident, as minute as it was, affected my outlook on nearly everything. If my mother said something, boy did my ears perk up. She taught me the importance of the consequences of my own actions. But the main thing was that my mother said what she meant, and did what she said. So now, when I work with these kids, sure I *may* cut them some slack, but they have to earn my respect. They have to know where I'm coming from and, more importantly, why. Either way, there is no doubt about my standards."

Another good example of the significance of someone's intentions was taught to the last emperor of China by his Western tutor, Reginald Johnston, who said, "Matter of words, perhaps, but words are important."

"Why are words important?" the child emperor inquired.

Without reservation the instructor wisely advised, "If you cannot say what you mean, Your Majesty, you will never mean what you say. And a gentleman should always mean what he says."

*   *   *

So whether you're the emperor of your palace, the president of your business, or the head of your household, it's your valued statements and the actions you take that give true meaning to your position.

And, as you are well aware, it is in fact the everyday, seemingly non-exciting, unassuming way you carry yourself that eventually places you head and shoulders above the majority of other individuals who couldn't *and* wouldn't care less.

In humdrum, everyday "real life" there may possibly be a time where some phenomenal, gigantic event occurs where you find yourself stepping into the breach, taking command, and assisting through leading. Where years of quiet self-discipline, training, and integrity are put to the ultimate test. Where again, living that seemingly boring lifestyle with those unwavering, outdated, old-fashioned values *now* suddenly becomes vital for others in need.

When newly elected mayor of New York City, Rudy Giuliani, was asked how he would combat the city's high crime rate, the mayor responded with a seemingly insignificant campaign, focusing on the scores of windshield washers who would dangerously scurry about at various traffic stops pandering for unsolicited services. When the mayor's office was besieged with objections such as "Why don't you go after murderers, or rapists and drug pushers?" the office in essence calmly responded, "We are going after *everyone* who breaks the law. If you do not have control over the smallest of infractions, you cannot tackle the bigger felonies."

It was only a few years later that this micromanaging

mayor of the Big Apple was dubbed Captain Courageous when he took control during the initial moments of the attacks on the World Trade Center. As bodies and debris rained from both towers, the mayor was nearly killed when a nearby building that he and his staff used as a command post collapsed. Yet, once outside, the mayor didn't skip a beat. He gave a quick survey of his surroundings and turned to his staff with the command, "*We* are our own country now. *We* must rely on ourselves. *We're* going to get through this. Let's take emotion out of the situation, do our job, save lives, and save this city."

During the course of that infamous day, among the chaos, among carnage, tens of thousands of ordinary citizens, in their own way, stepped up, pulled together, made extraordinary decisions, and took selfless actions that truly made a difference in the lives of so many.

Ordinary good folks making a true impact.

Again, there is maybe a one-in-a-million chance that a single opportunity will put your true character to the test, whether it be personal involvment in a war-like crisis, a life-or-death medical situation, or, God forbid, any other extreme personal tragedy. And if one cannot or will not back up what one says; if one lacks focus, discipline, integrity, and accountability in the small, seemingly insignificant things, how in heaven's name can a person summon the strength, the true grit, the courage to sacrifice and **do** (not just try to do) what has to be done?

Simply having words fly out of one's mouth at the speed

of sound is quite a feat, and for those who have an eloquent command of the language, I'm sure it's a musical treat to one's ears. But at the end of the day it takes more, particularly in this day and age, **so** much more. As the old adage goes, *actions* (your actions) speak louder than words.

Say It. Do It. Live It.

If we've discussed anything in this book, it's that all good things take time. Relationships, careers, health, finances, one's esteem: nothing happens overnight. Baby steps work the best. In your cause of self-improvement, or whatever your dedication, you set the bar by being consistent in your efforts. If you set a realistic, simple pace, gain your footing, build your confidence, earn sound experience, *then* and only then, you may be ready for the responsibility of leading others.

In a word, leadership is about *integrity*. Your integrity. For you and only you know in your heart of hearts what you've seen, all that you've experienced, and what is absolute. No games, no façades, no "acting," but the real you. Only you know the behind-the-scenes years of enormous, sweat-inducing time you've spent applying yourself, *while* all the time being proactive and dealing with all that life constantly throws in your lap. *Knowing who you **truly** are* should be enough.

And that's without feeling that you **must** tap-dance while balancing a pyramid of water glasses on your nose and belting out, "The hills are a-l-i-v-e with the sound of m-u-s-i-c," for an audience that doesn't even glance in your direction. That's without the need for you to feel you **must** endure the insults, the abuse, or the character assassinations.

Start accepting yourself for who you are and what you're about, including how you live your life.

Your integrity is about your personal standard, how you conduct yourself in all matters of your life. No matter how odd or how foolish it may seem to others, how you manage and live your life, your actions, and your standards should more than quiet that doubting Thomas in your head. If you're not satisfied, if you don't have the confidence, a strong confidence, in who you are and what you strive to achieve, how in the world do you expect others to accept you? How can you expect to set the example and set the pace if you do not believe in your most important asset? You!

For what it's worth, at this stage in your life, my advice to you is: It's you who knows you best. And if you don't, then *grow the hell up*, for you damn well should know yourself.

Take away, strip away, throw away your excuses, your façades, your defensive posturing, violin playing, cry me a river, and move it the heck along and start living life. No more bull, no more alibis, no more wasted time!

And with no disrespect to anyone, though spouses, close friends, and family members may know you intimately, only you have lived your entire life in your skin. You know your faults and your fears, your pride, and all your prejudices. Maybe you forgot, maybe you buried some things from those important childhood developmental years, but you know it was mostly those days, those experiences, those traumatic events, those happy times, that made you who you are today. The good, the bad, and the ugly: it's your life.

As Long as God Knows

Something was wrong.

"No," I replied after a moment, "I didn't say that. And that's certainly not what I meant. Sir."

As the nationally syndicated reporter simply shook his head, I wasn't sure whether he finally understood, agreed, or would deliberately take my response the wrong way.

"You hesitated." The man himself paused while raising an eyebrow. "Now, why would you do that?"

As tired as I was from dragging myself into the hotel at three in the morning only to show up for work just under four hours later, I still had enough sense to know something was not right. With every incoherent question that volleyed from all points of the compass, I found myself trying to justify every statement that came out of my mouth.

In hundreds of other interviews, I had told my story about what had happened and paid tribute to those who'd turned things around for me while also trying to convey a humble, yet universal, inspirational message. Even when digging into uncomfortable parts of my past, I made sure I was not over the top with the examples as well as doing my best to relieve pressure further by being relaxed myself.

But this interview was different. He was nothing like he had seemed during the numerous pre-interviews. On the phone, he had sounded kind, sincere, and genuinely interested in a grandfatherly way. Yet face to face, he appeared disconnected and arrogant, and seemed to feed off being combative. No matter what I said or how I tried to explain anything, he would instantly cut me off mid-sentence and turn everything around, or follow up with a rapid-fire question that had nothing to do with what he had just asked.

After a grueling, long, emotional day, followed by spending three hours on our second interview, I began to feel the strain. "So," he launched, "when you say sir, or ma'am, would you say that you use it as a guise—as a ruse, to dupe those you desire to feel sorry for you?"

"No, sir, I don't."

"Don't what?"

I took a different tack. "To me, saying sir or ma'am is second nature. I just do it to be polite. That's all. You know, random acts of kindness. Anyway," I deflected, hoping to put him back on track with the premise of the interview, "like I was saying before, that's the kind of service foster care provides. At least that's how my foster parents raised me."

Again, for the umpteenth time, the reporter brushed off my response with a wave of his hand. "Then you can't deny that you in fact entice others for pity? Is that it?"

"No," I huffed, shaking my head. "No, sir, that's not it at all."

"It's been my experience that those who seem excessively cordial have a different, premeditated agenda. It's usually to mask, to deflect from something quite different. What do you say to that?"

All I could do was smile back. "What you see is what you get."

"So you're saying you're genuinely polite?"

Unless you're an asshole, I said to myself.

"You come off as eager to please, too eager perhaps, in a simpleton golly gee-whiz Jimmy Olsen sort of way. Is that who you really are? I mean, I don't get it."

"Well, like anyone else, I have my moments—" I began to reply.

"You're rambling," he cut in as he scribbled down some notes.

I could only imagine him stating, when asked a direct question about what kind of person Pelzer really is, "He suddenly seemed dazed and confused . . ."

"Sir," I jumped in, swimming after him, "if I may, I'm only—"

Again came the wave-off. "All right, then, answer me this: What's it like to wake up one day to discover you're this raging overnight success? I gotta tell ya, I've been a freelance writer for well over twenty years and

I've written over a dozen books and all I get is rejection letter after rejection letter. So how come I can't get a deal, but someone—someone like you . . ."

"Um, I ah . . . don't . . . know." I stumbled. "Is this a personal question or part of the interview?"

The reporter raised his bushy eyebrow. "Hey now, don't get so defensive!" He barked for all the world to hear while snapping his head down to scribble on his notepad. When done, he flashed me a wry smile. "Hey, I'm just messin' with ya."

A long pause followed. I wanted to be polite. I wanted to have him see me as a good person. I wanted to accept his apology and apologize myself if I was out of line. Yet something told me stand fast, at least for . . .

After a few seconds, the reporter seemed agitated. "But, seriously, how'd ya do it? Come on, you can tell me—you came up with this idea and said, 'Hey, I'm gonna sell my little sob story for all the world to feel sorry for me. I'll get on *Oprah*, share my feelings. Get everyone to weep. Blame my parents, society for not understanding, then I can cash in.' Is that what you figured?"

Normally, I would have returned with a laugh, saying, "Yeah sure, you got me."

Then it hit me. No matter what I said or did, no matter my intentions or whatever dues I had paid, this guy was going to try to bury me! And the more I tried to justify myself in responding to his inquiries, the more it would appear to him that I was swimming after his approval.

The whole thing, the last few weeks before the interview of fulfilling endless requests: verifications from my teachers, foster parents, letters of reference from all across the globe, copies of commendations, even weekly updates of my book's latest standing on the *New York Times* Bestseller List, was a complete charade.

With my mind beginning to spin, my heart raced into overdrive. I still could not come to grips with what was now transpiring right in front of me. I was smarter than that. All I could do now was to appear unfazed and sit still while maintaining a neutral expression.

Like a fool, when the request for the interview came in I fell for the whole "I've been following your career for a while, young man. I see a story about a person who not only transcended, but who encourages those in the trenches of social welfare and gives more than mere hope to those in need. This is a story that needs to be told.

"So," the reporter went on, "there are those who say that you buy your books by the thousands just to make the bestseller list, then return them. What would you say to that?"

"No, sir."

"No what?"

"No, I have never done anything like that. And I would never even think of doing so," I flatly returned.

"But"—the reporter raised his hand while flipping through his notes—"I spoke to one of the bookstores where you recently did a signing, and you in fact purchased several books—"

Now I smiled inside. Without meaning to, he was revealing his hand. "Sir," I interjected, "when I learn that someone at one of my signings who goes out of their way to see me can't afford a book, I figure the least I can do is buy one for them. At a signing I may buy ten, twenty books at a time. Bottom line: I don't need to do that, I believe it's the right thing to do. But twenty books is certainly not going to put me on the bestseller list."

"Now, how would I know that?"

On the outside I remained neutral. Inside my head I stated, *If you were published, if you knew the field and how things really were, you would know.*

Before I could give an oral response, the reporter fired off, "Well, wouldn't you say that you've been rollin' in it now for some time? Come on, tell me, you go down to L.A., crash all those parties, trying to be the toast of the town and all? You like that, don't you?"

I wanted to jump from my chair and give him a piece of my mind. I worked hard, got lucky, and then worked harder and volunteered to travel all the more.

I didn't take the bait. By my silence I'm sure the nationally syndicated reporter sensed my shift. All I could do was sit still. From his fidgeting in his chair and flipping through his notepad I knew he was now out of his element. "But the book sales . . . that just doesn't happen," he stated.

"Well, it did," I volleyed back.

"Well, I know you could be making the big bucks on the motivational weekend or insurance-convention circuit. So why is it that you—"

I cut him off. "I don't need to. Sir."

"But you've got to have an angle. This Little Boy Blue thing—it just doesn't make sense to me."

I nodded in approval. "Well, what you see is what you get."

The reporter now flipped through his notes non-stop. He could tell I was ready to end our meeting. "But"—he raised a finger—"I, ah, I spoke to a relative, your grandmother, very feisty woman, who says that, that, your works were more like—and I quote—'more like fiction.'"

"Well." I sat back in my chair with my hands clasped together. "I've heard that before. And I think my office faxed you that exact statement from another interview from some time ago. Anyway, if even a fraction of what happened to me as a child were true, that in itself would be enough to have a kid pulled from the situation. On top of that, ask yourself this: At the time, when this happened, as you verified by speaking to my teachers as well as two of my foster parents—"

"I never said I called them," the reporter interjected.

"I believe you in fact did. Otherwise, why would one of my teachers and one of my foster parents call me complaining about how rude you were to them? Sir."

"Well . . ." he muttered without going any further.

After a solid beat I picked up where I'd left off. "Back then, when there were no laws, no penal codes to protect kids or those trying protect them—if I'm lying, then why was I suddenly removed, made a ward of the court, and placed in foster care?"

The reporter now seemed transfixed.

I lowered my voice to appear to be calmer than I truly felt. "I know I'm not the smartest guy in the room. And I know I still got a lot to learn. That I've made more mistakes than anybody—one of them being that I want to take people at face value, even though they have different, even sinister, agendas. I can't help that. Like me, hate me, disagree with me—whatever, it doesn't matter! What does is how I live my life. That I am a father to my son. That I'm not buried in some prison for committing unspeakable crimes, or out promoting chaos like the world's biggest terrorist. That I'm okay, in my golly-gee-whiz, Jimmy Olsen, Little Boy Blue way is, in fact, a tribute to the system—the teachers, the social workers, foster parents, and the host of others who not only put me on the right track, but saved my life.

"I know in my heart what is true. What's more important to me is that I know in my heart why I do what I do. And as long as I know and God knows, well then that's more than enough for me!

"Now with your permission, I gotta go and speak to some young adults who can use some positive guidance at the local juvenile hall."

"But I don't get it. Do you feel the need to . . . ? Why is it you do what you—"

I stood up and shook the reporter's now limp hand. "It doesn't really matter, now does it? Anyway, I know you're very busy. Thank you for your time. Good day . . . sir!"

Holding the Line

———— ‹◦› ————

- Rather than being steadfast in your critical beliefs at times when you find yourself being tested, do you often cave so as not to endure the "short-term" conflict? What effect does this have on maintaining your overall standards?

- What is your personal meaning of the word *integrity*? How do you live it?

- Do you find yourself trying too hard to gain the approval of others? If so, after all the time, energy, and expense you put into this, what exactly do you gain from your efforts?

- When being wrongly criticized by those who are deliberate in their ill actions, can you endure the situation while maintaining your dignity? What positive experience can you draw from the situation?

CHAPTER NINE

Living *Your* Life

Here it is: This whole thing, this little book, your life, your values are about *you*. How you carry yourself, the sum of your beliefs that make you strive to reach far beyond the norm and accomplish great deeds, are about living a life of true value. It's all about setting the tone for how you react, how you respond, how you lead in living *your* life.

For some who are passive and have little to no ambition, who deliberately scurry away from any form of responsibility because of cowardliness, afraid of making any ripples, life can be smooth sailing. But for others who might be a little scared and yet still have the backbone to stand up and be counted, who above all can be relied upon   for them, at times, waters can be rough.

Just be advised.

Don't forget that when you first begin to sail uncharted seas in the vast oceans of life, there is always that slight chance of falling off the edge of the earth. As you explore new worlds to better yourself and, more importantly, pilot others, you'll spend more time and energy fighting off mutinies than making headway in the mission you initially set out to accomplish.

In Your Face

The more you ascend and actually succeed in your life, the broader the impact you make on your cause, particularly in the lives of others. You'll find yourself being bombarded from all points of the compass. It's nearly unavoidable. Trust me, sooner or later it will come. It's almost like a twisted, never-before-seen *perfect storm*. It won't matter if you're just minding your own business, doing your own thing, and not looking for any praise. Even if you are, in fact, going out of your way *not* to draw any sort of attention to yourself, opposition, with all its slimy tentacles from the darkest of crevices, will try to attach itself to you and pull you under.

You'll also find opposition from those who have never taken a chance, who have never even thought about the mere idea of anything in the arena of productive, proactive accomplishments. Yet these individuals take the time to make the time. They go out of their way, as if it's their job, to be your most vocal opponent.

Why is that? Well, for some, they may feel threatened, jealous, or extremely ashamed of the lives they've led, or perhaps failed to have led.

Another reason some individuals go out of their way to act in a vengeful manner against you is because it makes them feel superior. They act in that manner in part so the light of disparity shines on them just a little less than it did before. It's their hope, and for some their mission, to put down and keep down others for the sole purpose of elevating their own worth. That's called *deflecting*. And that's not healthy.

For some it just may be that they are afraid of change. Very afraid. There can be a multitude of unknown reasons or excuses. Yet at the end of the day, does any of that really matter to *you*? Should you redirect your time, your attention, your resources to those who don't even have a mission, let alone the slightest hint of ambition? Why should you care what those with no integrity think about you and your honorable motives?

It shouldn't matter what others say or do when you're living your life, particularly if those people are toxic. But, as both of us know, in the reality of life it still affects us, gives us pause, and, sometimes, it still hurts. I'm talking deep down to the pit of your stomach kind of agony. Here you are, trying to make a difference, to make something of yourself, and **wham**, out of the blue, you take a punch in the midsection.

I can't begin to tell you how many thousands of times I've tried to reach out, sincerely tried to help out others when I didn't necessarily have to, and sometimes still gotten that finger in my face proclaiming that I didn't do enough, or that I wasn't quick enough to respond. At times I have heard horrible, horrible accusations. Even after all I've done, all I've been fortunate to accomplish, even to this day sometimes it still hurts.

I beg of you, trust me on this: If you've had a crappy past, if you've survived an unfortunate, even despicable, situation, as you now continue to reach out beyond the norm to better yourself, as you grow, you'll only become stronger. You'll only become all the wiser. So you damn well should be able to take a few jabs along the way. Come on, you can *so* do this.

Heck, when it comes to criticism, I say it's not all bad. If anything, it means you're making some sort of progress. While others are watching the world go by as they make their excuses, with their never-ending baby-like whining, warring with themselves to justify their own miserable lives, you are in fact accomplishing something. You are taking a stand for who you are and beliefs that you know to be true for you. So, tell me, how is that wrong? How is that bad, let alone *dis*honorable?

Again, maybe a squall or two isn't all that bad in the vast oceans of life.

Just give it some thought.

Look at it this way: Maybe a dig or two keeps you humble. Helps to ensure that you don't become too full of yourself. And the most important element is that those jabs and innuendos can actually aid you in evaluating your—ta-da: integrity.

Don't fret. Over time your skin will become a little bit thicker. As you grow your sensitive hearing will disseminate, break down, and filter out most of that vengeful, needless white noise.

Keep your head in the game. It's your life and your crusade.

Remember, whenever it comes to unwarranted attacks on your character, it's a game, but only if you play it.

All Too Human

Simply keep in mind that everybody takes a hit at some point. And I do mean E-V-E-R-Y-B-O-D-Y! There isn't a day in the paper, the television news, radio shows, or even that Internet headline banner scrolling on the top section of your computer screen that doesn't scream to the world how someone of stature did or *supposedly* did something that garnered attention.

We see it in the field of politics. As the election heats up, the underdog who suddenly becomes the front-runner gets hit by so many accusations that the politician's discussion about why he or she is running for office in the first place becomes completely mute in the fog of needless noise.

The same can be said for sports figures or celebrities. A year or so ago when these folks were coming up the ranks doing their own thing, we knew of them slightly but really didn't care about them all that much. But once they became "A-listers" traipsing down the red carpet, the finger pointing and character assassinations pound in non-stop waves.

Now to be fair, while some of these folks bring their follies entirely on themselves, some of them are in fact more than humble, appreciative, and live respectable, quiet lives.

My point being: None of us are immune—any parent, any chief executive officer, any supervisor, samaritan, visionary—anyone has more than his or her share of hits. The higher you climb, the more others will point their fingers at you. But, as with everything else, this is just one of the prices you will pay. It simply comes with the territory.

I am certainly no different. If that zany, over-the-top, redheaded comedian Kathy Griffin (whom I adore) is a D-list celebrity, I must, at best, be on the Z-list. Being of some notoriety for years now, there is rarely a week when I have not made someone mad to the point of hating me. It can stem from what I said or didn't say. What I did or didn't do. And it doesn't matter if I have gone way, way out of my way to clear my name, proving beyond any doubt that I was not in error. I discovered that this can only upset those certain individuals all the more.

I truthfully admit that sometimes, when I've been in the crosshairs, when I've been slammed so hard and with vicious intent, it pains me to my core. It's partly my pride and ego that make me discouraged, which I know is completely, utterly foolish.

Now I also freely acknowledge that I can rub some individuals the wrong way. I certainly don't mean to. And I never, absolutely never, do anything for the deliberate purpose of making others upset. I love nothing more than praising those who make a difference in the lives of others, while I assist where I can to make folks feel good about themselves. I do whatever I can to help open a door, any door, that may lead others to rediscover their self-worth and happiness. In a nutshell *that's* it! That's what I do. That's what *I* stand for.

Many years ago (boy, do I feel old!), I was presenting in the Northwest part of the United States and I nearly ignited a fire storm when I kept saying the word "ladies." The first time I said the word, as in, "Ladies and gentlemen," I received a vengeful look from the back part of the room. Half an hour later, when I repeated the word, a very young woman shot up and announced, "I'm no lady. You hear me? I'm no f——n' lady!"

Ya think?

After screeching her displeasure at my old-world, female-oppressing, sexist ways to the crowd, she and her female friend stomped out in front of a stunned crowd of hundreds. A week later I received a seven-page hate letter from the young gal telling me how I had not only ruined her day, but I had totally crushed her spirit. That I was the reason women still fought against dominating pigs such as myself and how people like me deserved nothing less than to rot in the depths of hell. The letter ended with a postscript describing not only that she would sue me, but also how much in damages she would seek from the overwhelming mental anxiety I had inflicted.

Wow!

I read the letter dozens of times, only to dissect it further. Not to sound dramatic, but I felt so horrible that I fell to my knees. I cried. I prayed. I battled with myself, thinking, *If I'm*

*making one person so enraged, I can only imagine how upset I must have
made tens of thousands of others.*

For weeks I allowed that situation and that spiteful letter
to dominate my thoughts. For weeks I thought of nothing
else. It tore me up. I lost sleep. I could barely keep anything
down. Yet, as I began to calm down and after seeking sound,
honest advice, I was finally able to get a single night's sleep.
It took a little more time for me to come to the realization
that it wasn't the end of the world. I searched my heart
knowing full well that while I accepted responsibility for
my words and deeds, I had been, in fact, only going out of
my way to be polite to the audience. I then recalled that for
many, many years I'd said the same word thousands upon
thousands of times with no ill effects, absolutely none whatsoever, which eventually helped me with my introspection
all the more. Only then, after I looked at the entire matter
for *what it was,* did I begin to feel better—cleaner—about
myself.

Being that this was my first major hit, when I next appeared onstage, I hesitated. I felt guarded. Most of all, I felt
hampered that I couldn't, wouldn't, give my all. It began to
eat at me that I was not being *me.*

And that's not right either. For any of us to constantly
knee-jerk at every encounter with narrow-mindedness, to
completely change direction at the whims of others for
the sole purpose of *possibly* not offending, I say that's just
plain stupid. That's not leadership and it's certainly not
displaying one's integrity. If anything, it's cowering in

cowardliness. Therefore, I say when you take your stance, be of true heart. Keep your chin up and your eyes open to backlash. Again, it all comes with the real estate of learning.

Now, I have absolutely no problem with altering a plan, receiving sound critiques, or making an occasional course correction. If I can do something that can help me become more effective, I'm more than willing, at the very least, to consider the possibility.

About ten years have passed since that difficult encounter, and now when I look back at the situation I can view the experience as a positive building block. Like all of us, I have made and will continue to make mistakes, some of them absolutely, stupidly outrageous. At least for me, especially with my luck, it's nearly unavoidable, in part because I'm always stretching beyond a set comfort zone. Mistakes also keep me from becoming too complacent or unappreciative. So now when I receive deliberate hate-filled statements, I look at the source, offer them a quiet, quick prayer, and move it along. If anything, the ultra-hyper, supersensitive, always-whining, do-nothing-but-complain club makes me more determined in my mission.

So even to this day, does it still hurt? Oh yeah! And in some ways I think it should. Because it shows that we still have feelings, that we're not too jaded or think we're above it all. That all of us are, in fact, human. You're never going to be able to change how some individuals think or how they act. It's a hard but basic part of the reality of life. All I can do, all you can do, is go about your business, doing all that you can to the best of *your* abilities.

So to heck with them.

Same Scenario, Different Attitude

Does the scrutiny ever go away? Oh no, if anything it just keeps piling on.

Just a short time ago I returned to the northwestern part of the nation, to the same city where the "l" word incident took place, and—guess what? Lo and behold, I set off a few folks. As I gave the presentation I knew I was swimming up-river against the white rapids without a paddle. As much as I tried, I felt I wasn't connecting all that well. But just the same, I gave it all I had. It wasn't until weeks later that I received another letter—telling me I had screwed up, again.

As my business director, Gabbi, laid down the letter in front of me, she warned, "Now don't spin. Don't go crazy, but this is something you have to read."

My crime of the century, among other things, was saying "God bless you." As in "If you're helping others, God bless you" and "If you're in a dark place where things aren't going your way and you still have the courage to get up every day and face your demons against all odds and still function and contribute to society, then God bless you" and "If you need a little encouragement, a little boost in morale, well, may God bless you."

As I reread the letter, I could feel my stomach tighten. My head slowly began to spin out into orbit. I instantly knew

I could allow this correspondence to eat me up. Or I could simply act as if I had never read it, let alone received it, therefore not caring one iota. *Or*, I quietly thought to myself, *I could do something.*

I snatched up the phone and spoke to the sponsor for the event. After a few pleasantries, I eased in with "Thank you for taking the time to write me. I personally read your letter and—" Suddenly, the lady's tone changed entirely from warm to cold and defensive. "You must understand—we all must be sensitive to all people's feelings. Some—not *all*, mind you—but some were taken aback by some of your comments."

"Well," I replied, "first off, I truly apologize. That was never my intention."

Still in a guarded voice, the lady, whose attitude was now totally different from when she'd happily chatted with me hours before the program, jumped in with, "I can feel the meaning of your words; however, you did say that, *that statement* seven times. To some—not all, but to some—they may have, well, possibly taken your comments as a way of endorsing a certain persuasion. You have to understand the sensitive times we live in. You of all people should know how words can ignite a response."

Of course, without thinking, without meaning to, while still holding the phone, I accidentally blurted out, "Seven times? I said 'God bless you' seven times in ninety minutes? Wow! Usually I say it more. A lot more."

"And your humor," she continued. "While many may

have laughed at your wit and impersonations, I really don't think the audience quite expected you to be that amusing. That might have confused them. Which can only add to them feeling uncomfortable."

"But ma'am," I replied, "I'm confused. Did we not meet two hours before the program, when I asked about incorporating humor to loosen the folks up, because **you** told me the folks had had several days of extensive training and needed a break? Did I not ask **you** about my saying the exact words *God bless*? Wasn't I, in fact, very specific, asking you what **you** wanted me to do?"

"I'm not quite certain if I recall receiving you before the presentation. I'm very busy. I don't have time to sort out every issue," the lady reluctantly scoffed. "And I do not see how any of this is relevant. Someone like yourself should dedicate more time to becoming more sensitive to the needs of others, so not to be offensive."

"Ma'am, please. I'm really trying to understand. I am in no way trying to shirk my responsibilities. If I screwed up, it's on my shoulders and mine alone. But I don't know what it is exactly you want me to do."

From the other end of the line I could hear the lady tap her fingernails. After a long pause she cleared her throat. "Well, to begin with, you should state your intentions, including your humor, in your materials that you send out before anyone contracts your services."

"We do. We've done that since I first started. That's standard procedure."

"Then perhaps you should redo it, in bigger print. You need to consider that not everyone has time to read them. I also think you need to submit a full-length document of your presentation to enable a panel to evaluate and make required corrections. Then you would resubmit for further corrections until the panel becomes satisfied. Or"—the lady snapped her fingers—"it would be most beneficial for others if you could fly in, spend a few days, give your complete presentation for consideration, then the panel would have direct input on how they feel."

"Ma'am"—I almost gawked at the phone in my hand—"are you serious? Do you require or would you even ask this of anybody else?" I queried, trying to make an off-hand but obvious point.

"Of course not. Now that would be just plain silly," she huffed, as if I should have known. "But you're different. You're Dave Pelzer."

Gaining stride, the lady blitzed on to express a better course of action: In order not to take the chance of igniting folks, I **should** immediately cancel every future appearance (yes, she actually said this—no kidding), stay off the road for about a year, and my team and I should scour every document, every taped interview, to analyze and dissect anything that may possibly be considered offensive. She then continued that I should use the time as a deep meditative awakening experience to understand the sensitivity of being, well . . . more sensitive.

All-righty-then!

Yet, in real life, what made the conversation so outrageous, so maddening, was how sincere and how adamant the lady was. Even when I chided, "Gosh, a whole year? And mainly 'cause I said *God bless* five, six times?"

With a sudden rush of air, she quickly blurted, "Seven! You said *that* statement seven times."

All I could do was nod my head. "Well, next week I'm scheduled to go overseas to Iraq and speak to the troops. It's a huge honor. I've been ask to do some jokes, tell a few stories, offer some encouragement. But, if I'm that offensive, well . . . maybe I shouldn't go."

Without skipping a beat, without even considering the magnitude of being "sensitive" to what I had just said, let alone "my" feelings, the lady chimed, "That sounds like a very positive step. I'm sure that would be for the best. Again, we should all be aware of the sensitive times we live in."

"But," I chimed, "if we don't speak out, if we don't act upon what's in our hearts, if our intentions are true and forthright, how is that such a bad thing? If we don't take a chance, how can we strive for progress? If we cower and cave in to every itty-bitty thing, if we change ourselves, our attitudes, our core beliefs for the sole sake of appeasement, how does that make anything better? What does that say about our values? What does that say about our integrity?"

I stumbled on. "If these are in fact *sensitive* times, should we not be sensitive and respect everyone's—and I mean *everyone's*—feelings, beliefs, and intentions, including my own? I apologize for screwing up, for upsetting those folks. Truly

I do. But I don't believe that saying *God bless* a few times, eulogizing, praising those who make a difference, and stressing the importance of resilience and personal accountability is a bad thing or makes me a bad guy. **I am** sensitive to the needs of others, and it's because of that *and* my beliefs that I'm asked to present.

"In the future I will be more aware and sensitive, but overall I pride myself for at least going 'out there' and taking a chance at making things better, rather than doing little to nothing by keeping my head down and eyes shut, hoping not to upset the status quo."

"Well, you don't have to be so, so—"

"Sensitive?" I broke in.

"I was only suggesting that you should take a year . . ." The lady trailed off after catching her breath. "I can certainly feel what you are saying. Of course you are allowed to feel as you wish. Perhaps, in the end, time will tell."

Knowing I had overstepped my bounds, I genuinely thanked the lady for her time and her critique. Then I rocketed my foot back into my mouth by uttering those three infamous words that had started this whole escapade.

"God bless you."

On the other end, all I could hear was labored breathing before the line suddenly went dead.

Dear reader, please understand, there are times, rare instances, when I am conversing, when I am expressing a sound, deep, philosophical meaning, that the words pour out of my mouth like water from a purified crystal well. When those eloquent moments happen I feel like Cary Grant, Peter O'Toole, or Will Rogers. Yet, unfortunately, *most* of the time, I'm the stammering, stuttering, blathering village idiot. No matter how hard I try, how much I study, it's simply in my nature to botch it up.

Thinking about the conversation now, as I scribe these words to you, maybe placing that call was not the wisest thing for me to have done. While I admit that part of it was my ego, I primarily did it to discover my true errors, and in the end it became more of a passionate crusade for my credibility.

The main reason I went into embarrassing detail in the preceding example is for you not only to be aware that inescapable critiques will come your way, but also to let you know that, as you excel, sometimes your convictions **will** be judged according to unfair and unachievable standards by one-sided individuals, and that the least of your errors can be and will be magnified a thousand times against you.

Tack it up. For this is all part of the price of leadership and living.

Screwups are unavoidable, an obvious fact of life. And you will never, ever come close to satisfying the minority of the masses. However, what should never be in doubt is your integrity. Your honor.

Give pause and analyze the situation? You bet! Tuck your tail between your legs in response to your sound efforts and compromise your righteous values so that, maybe, possibly, you won't displease others? Hell no!

Understand that we all want to be wanted, to be loved and respected. We all want to be right all the time. But that's not possible, nor is it normal. It's good to adjust. It's healthy to make corrections when needed. That should never stop. It's called progress! But to chase after those who are so lost in space at the far regions of another solar system, making senseless, contemptible *critiques* while not even considering your position is way, way beyond asinine.

In my case, I tried to be nice and considerate to the sponsor. As anyone, especially someone like myself, should. I know that the more I travel and the more recognition I receive, the more my head is going to be on the chopping block. It's a fact I've come to accept. But the more I listened, trying to dissect and prove my points, the more I knew I was being sucked into a black hole. I thought that offering apologies, gently stating my position, should have been enough.

What I should have done was end the conversation way before the lady had dreamed up the notion of me combing through and reviewing presentations from ten and fifteen years ago. And I certainly should have halted the discussion before she went on to patronize my upcoming overseas trip to pay tribute to America's finest. Bottom line: *I should not have allowed the situation to get that far.*

I certainly won't allow future situations to get so out of control, so bizzare. But, as you now know about me, my luck, my life, and my mouth—odds are it's inevitable. At least with this one episode I stood my ground more than I ever did years before. I did not completely concede. Nor did I bow in the direction of the winds for that particular moment for the sole reason of another's opinion.

Personally and professionally speaking, the most significant element I drew from the whole experience, whether it be the malicious, hate-filled letter or the conversation itself, was that I did not permit either one to devour my soul. And I never even contemplated throwing in the towel.

As I have stated, and as you have read, there are those who seem to leap out from nowhere pointing the finger of wrath in your face. Those are the same individuals with whom you try to make amends, to whom you try at least to express your views, and still it's never enough. Even though their stance is as solid as Jell-O, the only time they may display any sign of having a backbone is when they insist that you darn well better jump on their bandwagon, tout de suite.

There are those who blunder through life accommodating, hoping to keep that low profile and fly below the radar. They hope, they pray, and, with all their might, they try not to ruffle any feathers, not to make any ripples in the smallest of ponds. And I'm sure that plan probably works out well for some. Whether it's the irate finger-pointers who love nothing more than to criticize or those hiding in their cocoon, ask yourself, What do they contribute? What do they bring to the table? Is there anything *they* have said or actually accomplished that is of any credence, any value whatsoever?

From the tallest mountain I'll shout for all to hear, "**God bless!** God bless those who try. Good for you for having the guts to take a stand." *That's what I believe, so that's how it is.*

I say whether they like you, love you, despise you, or loathe you, **hold your ground**. Do not concede your values. Do not shiver in the darkest shadows wondering, *What if? I wonder if I should have, could have, tried to do that one thing.*

If you have something to offer, if you have something to contribute, then step up. "Mr. President, Madam Secretary, I truly don't believe that is the correct course of action at this time. You may wish to consider . . ."

At the same time, when someone addresses you with "Supervisor Smith" or "Ms. Jones" or "Mom, you promised" or "You said" or "You didn't do," take the jab to the chin, admit your error, and move it along.

Trust me when I say that in any case, by stepping up to the boss at work or having your shortcomings brought up to you by your kids, it will be completely forgotten in a matter of hours, days, weeks, or months at the very most. However, what will be remembered, what will follow you everywhere, is your integrity, your values, and your beliefs.

We all have to and should continue to adjust, be accommodating and well mannered *as needed*. It's a necessity of life. So when—not if, but when—you take one on the chin for screwing up, don't take it too personally; realize that it's not the end of the world and adjust. Unless it's something drastic, I recommend that, for the most part, you stay the course.

When you pull the reins in on the kiddies or know-it-all, want-it-all, be-all teens, when the door slams after they screech: "You have no right! It's not fair! I hate you!" Not to worry. While those of inexperience and immaturity dance around you losing their cool and all self-control, you, being a person who knows your way around, keep your temper in check and under total control. While other kids are "out there" doing Lord knows what at all hours, your babes are stewing away, doing their homework in the safety of their cozy little rooms. As you know, when it comes to parenting, you can cave in now in order to avoid "dealing with it," or take the occasional rap to the jaw to maintain the long-term vision of raising productive, responsible, happy adults.

If anyone at work or in other places is callous, overly corrective, or stupidly hypersensitive to your convictions, work ethics, or optimistic outlook on life, pay no heed. Remember, as an independent, responsible, reasonable adult you are the captain of your own destiny. You man your own helm. Just keep your eyes on the upcoming triumphant horizon.

All Around Us

Opportunities for greatness are rare. Yet, despite all that swirls around us throughout life, we muster to the challenge. The more we refuse to bend to the prevailing wind, the more opportunity for greatness can become an everyday occurrence. Really, it's all in the standards of how one lives one's life. You should know where you stand and how to react *before* any event develops. Before you set sail, you should at the very least unfold your chart and plot your own course. You should know and accept that when you step into the ring, you're going to take some hits.

The taller you stand, the more others emerge from their

snakeholes and with their axes. Some wait for a precise moment to cut you down. Others will just stand around with anticipation, waiting and hoping to see you fall over.

Not to worry. Stand tall. Hold the line. Remember that in life bad-weather surges are unavoidable. Yet it's the tree with the deepest of roots that has in fact weathered the velocity of the worst storms.

You will be just fine!

Epilogue

W ell, God love ya, you did it. You made the commitment, you "cowboyed up," and you followed
through. Good for you! I'm so proud!

To me, in a word, to step up and follow through means
resolve. To me, it also means to have purpose, to have and
maintain determination. Hmm . . . after reading this book,
do those words remind you of anyone? Does the meaning now help crystallize who you are, what you wish to
accomplish, and why you should keep your faith in your
mission?

As in my life, when I set out on a new writing project I
have a plan. As I have jokingly said a zillion times, "When
man plans, God laughs." All in all, the more I worked on
this book for you, the more I had to dig deeper than I initially intended. Did you find that, as you were reading (and,
I hope, absorbing) parts of this book, it tapped into aspects
and maybe a few incidents in your life?

My point being: You were never alone in your beliefs or
your determination to do better, to move your life forward.

Epilogue

And now that you're done with this book, ask yourself, *How do I feel?* Do you feel relieved? More resolved? A little bit more at ease, or even clearer about yourself? At the very least, you damn well should!

As your author and guide, I know I can be a little overwhelming. That's my job: to shake you up and get you to open up and reexamine your life and its priorities. And you know as well as I do that, as much as I may have challenged you, you never, ever would have read a portion of this book unless you truly wanted to turn that corner in this part of your life.

So now it's all up to you. Just like this book, as intense as it is, life comes at you pretty fast. I highly recommend that you now relax. Take some time, digest, and reevaluate things. Then, when you're ready, as you go off into the unknown, take baby steps. You may be afraid. Be advised that this is completely normal. But the more you stretch beyond yourself, the more you'll grow. It doesn't matter how far you go or how long it takes; as long as you're "out there" doing something, that's A-okay by me and anyone else who truly cares. Bottom line: Don't you worry.

Some time ago Father Lincoln, the senior pastor of my church, said this: "There are times when my works are put in doubt. That others point the finger of despair in my direction. But as long as I know who I am, why I do what I do, and as long as God knows, well then, to heck with everybody else."

As I have said countless times, directly or indirectly, in

the end it is all about faith. Faith in yourself and faith in your mission.

If you continue to challenge yourself, if you continue to move forward, and if you continue to remain steadfast in your convictions, I swear to you, with my hand on the Bible, you will prevail. It may take time and you may endure a few raps to the chin, but if you carry on, at least you are righteous in your cause. At this stage in your life, after reading this book, tell me—or, better yet, tell yourself—what other choice you have but to move forward.

Please take the following quote to heart. It may be a little dramatic and not fit every situation you'll deal with, but, personally speaking, when I feel my back's against the wall, or when I just want to pack it all in, this one saying is my saving grace: "All that is necessary for evil to succeed is that good men do nothing." That statement was powerful back in the 1700s when Edmund Burke first stated it. Today, in a post-9/11 era when tens of thousands of families work themselves to the bone to make ends meet, that statement resonates all the more. All of us are called to take off our blinders, step up and out of our protective womb, say it like it is, regain our focus and our drive toward what truly matters, and do what needs to be done!

Get it?

As I close, let me state that it has been an honor to serve with you! Thank you for taking a chance and spending time on this book. With all my heart, I pray for your success and for your happiness.

Epilogue

Work hard, be kind, and help others along the path of life. Be happy, and be happy now! Damn it!

As I say on my radio show, "Peace is always within you; always be in peace. So until next time, my friend, good day, good luck, and, as always, God bless!"

ABOUT THE AUTHOR

A retired air force air crew member, Dave played a major role in Operations Just Cause, Desert Shield, and Desert Storm. Dave was selected for the unique task of midair refueling of the once highly secretive SR-71 Blackbird and the F-117 Stealth Fighter. While serving in the air force, Dave worked in juvenile hall and other programs involving "at-risk" youth throughout California.

Dave's exceptional accomplishments include commendations from Presidents Ronald Reagan, George H. W. Bush, Bill Clinton, and George W. Bush, as well as various other heads of state. While maintaining an international active-duty flight schedule, Dave was the recipient of the 1990 J.C. Penney Golden Rule Award, naming him the California Volunteer of the Year. In 1993, Dave was honored as one of Ten Outstanding Young Americans (TOYA), joining a distinguished group of alumni that includes Chuck Yeager, Christopher Reeve, Anne Bancroft, John F. Kennedy,

About the Author

Orson Welles, and Walt Disney. In 1994, Dave was the only American to be selected as one of The Outstanding Young Persons of the World (TOYP), for his efforts involving child-abuse awareness and prevention, as well as for instilling resilience in others. During the centennial Olympic games, Dave was a torch bearer, carrying the coveted flame. Dave is also the recipient of the 2005 National Jefferson Award, which is considered the "Pulitzer Prize" for public service. Other recipients include Sandra Day O'Connor and former Secretary of State Colin Powell.

Dave is the author of six other inspirational books including: *A Child Called "It,"* which was on the *New York Times* bestseller list for more than six years. He is one of only a few authors to have four #1 international bestsellers, and to have four books simultaneously on the *New York Times* bestseller list. He is currently working on his next book, titled *Too Close to Me.*

Dave is also the host of *The Dave Pelzer Show,* heard weekly on VoiceAmerica internet radio at www.voice.voiceamerica .com. Dave would love to hear from you and invites you to call in live. For details, you can visit his Web site and click on "Radio Dave."

When not on the road or with his son, Stephen, Dave lives a quiet life in Southern California with his box turtle named Chuck.

You can visit Dave's Web site at www.davepelzer.com.

Dave is a living testament of resilience, faith in humanity, and personal responsibility. Dave's unique and inspirational outlook on life, coupled with his Robin Williams–like wit and sense of humor, entertains and encourages business professionals to overcome any obstacle while living life to its fullest. This is what makes him one of the most exceptional and unequalled personalities in the public-speaking arena today.

Dave also provides specific programs to those who work in the human services and educational fields.

For additional information on having Dave for your group, you can call, fax, or visit his Web site at

D-ESPRIT
P.O. Box 1846
Rancho Mirage, CA 92270

Phone: 760-321-4452
Fax: 760-321-6842
www.davepelzer.com